ESSENTIALS
of Strategic Project Management

Kevin R. Callahan
Lynne M. Brooks

WILEY

John Wiley & Sons, Inc.

Library of Congress Cataloging-in-Publication Data:

Callahan, Kevin R.
  Essentials of strategic project management / Kevin R. Callahan, Lynne M. Brooks.
      p. cm.
  Includes index.
  ISBN 0-471-64985-6 (paper/Web site)
  1. Project management. I. Brooks, Lynne M. II. Title.
  HD69.P75C35 2004
  658.4' 04—dc22

                                                            2004005517

To Larry Jarres for his words of wisdom, strategic outlook, and his faith in our business skills and abilities.

To Catherine for putting up with me.

To Sheila for always being there.

Contents

Preface

Companies are always trying to find better ways to get things done. Over the last few years, there has been a movement to improve project management at many companies. They will spend a great deal of time, expense, and effort identifying project managers, developing programs, and delivering training. The problem is that after all of this effort nothing changes and the executives of these companies wonder why.

Implementing project management at a company is difficult for many reasons. Change itself is difficult. Project management is much more than a series of tools and techniques for individual project managers to master. However, the most important reason that implementing project management is difficult is that *companies do not understand the strategic nature of project management!* If project management and its related areas of expertise—portfolio management and project office—are not seen by executives and managers as *strategic tools* that are directly related to their companies' bottom lines, then they will not be able to implement project management successfully.

This book is primarily intended for executives who need to learn the basics of project management to enable them to make decisions about implementing or improving project management at their company. It is also useful to any individual who needs a basic introduction to project management. In this book, readers will learn

- What project management, project portfolio management, and a project office are and how they are affected by an organization's structure

- How project management tools and techniques can be best used at their company

- How to use a proven model to break down the barriers to strategic project management within their company

Chapter 1 and 2 will introduce readers to the problems that face many firms and how project management can help them solve those problems. Chapters 3 through 5 cover the basics of the five phases of project management: initiation, planning, execution, control, and closing. In particular, these chapters address the problems that different types of organizations will face in implementing each of the project management phases. Chapters 6 and 7 introduce project management maturity and the project office, respectively. Chapter 8 discusses project portfolio management and also explains how to put it all together.

The book is filled with practical tips as well as comprehensive explanations of critical path calculation and earned value management that will help the reader to understand what they are and why they are important. Also available is a Web site (*www.wiley.com/go/pm*) containing practical project tools that may be downloaded and used by the readers.

Acknowledgments

We would like to thank all of the many people who have supported us as we have written this book. First of all, to the inspiration, Mike Hugos, who both moved us to write and encouraged us to do so. Mike also spent a great deal of time proofreading our work and making valuable suggestions. We offer a special thanks to Trey Hickman, for keeping our ideas in the real world.

We would like to thank our researchers, Erin Mills and Alex Vorros, for dedicated hours and for making sure that we did not miss anything. Thanks to all of those who have shared their experience with us: Marianne Mertes, Artell Smith, Julie Brubaker, Bill Barnett, and Mike Shires.

We would be remiss if we did not thank our editor, Tim Burgard, for trusting us and for showing us the ropes.

Finally, to all of those who are too numerous to name (and whose names we would not want to forget) for the interest they have shown in us and in our careers.

About the Web Site

This book includes a companion Web site available at *www.wiley.com/go/pm*. The Web site contains forms and templates you can use as tools for better project management. The files in the Web site are as follows:

- Communications Planning Template
- Project Decision Worksheet
- Project Prioritization Analysis
- Project Status Report
- Project Summary Report
- Scope Change Control Form
- Strategic Project Charter Template
- Strategic Project Charter Checklist
- Task-Definition Form

For more information and tool updates, visit *www.thepmci.com*.

CHAPTER 1

The Problem with Project Management

After reading this chapter you will be able to

- Understand why so many projects are not successful
- Understand how knowledge, expertise, and process are the keys to change
- Understand the STO model and the problems it illustrates
- Be able to use this book as a tool in understanding project management

A Story From the Frontlines

Frank Coleman, the Vice President of Operations at ABC Corp., approached his office. It was Monday, 6:00 A.M. Frank usually came in very early, because it was the only time he could get any work done without being interrupted. He knew before he rounded the corner into his office what he was going to see. Sure enough, stuck to his monitor, keyboard, chair, and desk were several dozen yellow notes. He placed his briefcase next to his desk and noticed the flashing light on his phone—a sure sign his voice mailbox was full again. Frank took the notes off his chair and cleared a path on his keyboard and monitor. He would look at all the notes later. Frank ran his hands through his hair and sank into his chair. He drew in a deep breath and let it out slowly as he logged into ABC's intranet. After the usual login messages flashed by, the e-mail

1

system displayed 150 unread messages, at least half of which began with the word URGENT. Frank groaned, leaned back in his chair, and closed his eyes.

For Frank, this was the normal start of any day—problems and more problems. For the first time this day, he wondered why people here couldn't solve more of their own problems. His priorities were clear; as a member of the leadership team, he wanted his people to get things done on the projects that were assigned to them, but nobody seemed to be able to do that. There were just too many projects!

He opened his briefcase and took out a pile of papers that he had been working on and found the Thompson file. He really needed to finish his review of the client proposal today. He wondered if Stevens had completed the resource estimates that he needed for this proposal. He really did not want to wade through e-mail right now to find them, so he continued working on another part of the proposal. Even as he did so, in the back of his mind he wondered where they would find the resources to do this project for the client. He would have to hire new people and increase his budget. How was he ever going to justify that? If only his people could be more productive.

As the thought struck him, Frank sat back in his chair and reflected. What else could he do to get his people to be more productive? They had already spent a small fortune buying and implementing that new enterprise-wide project management tool, and they had trained everybody on how to use it. Yet, he still could not get a simple progress report once a month, let alone once a week, that he could understand and share with the CEO and CFO.

A sharp, tense voice startled him. "Got a minute, Frank?" It was Bob Jenkins. "Sure, Bob. What's up?" he answered, knowing full well what Bob was going to say next. On Friday afternoon he had transferred two people from Bob's project team to another project after Paul Bruce complained that his project was going to miss an important deadline if he did not get more resources.

"Frank, how can you expect me to get anything done if you keep taking all of my resources away? I'm down three resources since my project began, and we were understaffed to begin with. We are already on the verge of being late and this will push us over the edge! You know that Deakins is one of our biggest accounts. If we don't deliver on time this time, we may lose this account. Just what am I supposed to tell them when we meet on Wednesday? Two fewer bodies around the table won't go unnoticed."

Frank took another deep breath as he considered what to say to Bob. He really wanted to tell him to figure out a way to get things done himself, but he knew that would only make Bob angrier. He understood that Bob needed the resources he had shuffled, but he did not have any extra resources to spare. Which project should he shortchange next? Perhaps the Jones project could spare some people. No, they had missed a deadline last month and could well miss one this month even if they kept all of their people. How about XYZ Company? No, he had talked to Gina about that a couple of weeks ago; they had no people to spare either. Wait a minute! There were three people tied up on the internal HR payroll project If they moved back the schedule on that one, it would not impact any clients. He would get the extra resources from HR to placate Bob. He would just have to deal with Marge Betters, the Vice President of Human Resources. He would worry about that later.

"Frank! Did you hear what I just said?"

"I heard you, Bob. I was just trying to figure out what to do. I'm sorry that I had to move those people on Friday, but the Osterly project had a real emergency. I know they wound up working all weekend. I might be able to replace those resources. Are you sure you can't just make do with the resources you have for the time being?"

"Make do? I told you, we were behind before you started taking away all of my people."

"And why is that, Bob? I gave you all the resources that you said you needed when you started the project. What went wrong?"

"It wasn't our fault. The people over at Deakins didn't get their requirements to us until two weeks after the deadline. With cooperation like that, what am I supposed to do?"

"All right, Bob, I'm making no promises, but I will try to find additional people for your team."

"Okay, Frank, but the sooner the better. Oh, by the way, you need to know that people are really getting upset these days. The people you moved to the Osterly project were frustrated at getting the call to work all weekend on a Friday. They're not the only ones. We've got a lot of people who are unhappy; every time they turn around, they're on a new project. They don't have any idea what we're expecting them to do. There's a lot of grumbling going on."

"Okay, see what you can do with the rewards program to make them feel better, but they are just going to have to get used to it for a while. The hiring freeze really ties my hands."

Frank thought he could not be too tough on Bob; he worked hard and seemed to be at the office night and day. It was not like Bob was sloughing off or anything. He would call the head of the HR project with the bad news when he had a moment. Frank returned to the Thompson file and continued working. This time, he was lucky, and no one interrupted him for 30 minutes. Occasionally, as he was working, he heard the telephone ring, but he ignored it. For some reason, when it rang around 8:15 he glanced up to see who it was and picked up the receiver.

"Frank Coleman."

"Frank, it's about time you picked up the phone." It was Amanda Stevens, VP of Manufacturing at Bigelow Company.

"Morning, Amanda, how are you?"

"Not very happy," snapped Amanda. "Did you know that we have not received the prototype of the new widget that you are designing for us?'

Why didn't he know that? If his people could not use the new project management tool to report their status, couldn't they at least warn him when there was a problem?

"Amanda, I am pushing them to get it to you ASAP." Well, at least he would, once he got off the telephone and could get down to Perry Smith's department to find out what was going on. They had better have a good reason for missing the deadline.

"You know, Frank, we have been very good clients of yours for over ten years, but the way you handle things lately is unacceptable. We can occasionally handle delays, but the real problem is that we never hear from your people at all. We don't know what is going on until it's too late. Instead of an asset, you are becoming a liability and a huge risk for us. In the case of this widget, we already have our production and marketing plans in place, are setting up equipment, and bringing new people on. This delay could cost us serious money, and if it does, it will cost you money as well!"

Frank reassured Amanda. "If it comes down to that, we'll make it right." And if it came to that, Frank also knew that he would have an angry CEO and CFO to deal with.

"I'll tell you what Amanda, I will take a walk down to the proto-type group, see what's up, and call you back."

"You'll call me back today? Is that a promise?"

"As soon as I know something, I will call you."

"Okay, I expect to talk to you later," and Amanda abruptly hung up.

Frank shot out of his chair and headed downstairs toward the proto-type team. Halfway there, he looked at his watch and realized that he had a meeting with Jim Barnett, the CEO, in five minutes. "It will have to wait until after my meeting," Frank muttered. As he reversed direction, he almost ran into Maria Dellarme. Like everyone else he had encountered so far this day, Maria did not look happy.

Maria scowled at Frank. "Did you approve the new vendor contract that the Meridian plant project is using? This is going to cost us a ton of money. You know we have a hiring freeze on, and you can't get around that by hiring vendors instead of employees. If you need resources, you'll just have to wait until the freeze is over and I can approve the hiring of new employees for the project."

"Actually, I did approve it," he told Maria, his tone rising as well. "Without those resources, we can't finish all this work that has to be done. The contract is signed; we'll just have to deal with it. Look, Maria, I have a meeting to get to right now. When it's over, I will give you a call."

"Well, all right," Maria said, "but it's your budget that's going to be busted!"

Frank had forgotten about the contract. He had meant to go and talk to Maria about it but had never gotten around to it. "Just what I need, another fire to put out today." He was already ten minutes late.

Frank rounded the corner to the executive suite at a jog. Marge, the CEO's administrator, just looked at him and gestured to Jim's door. Jim hated when people were late for meetings.

Jim was on the phone with his back to the door when Frank walked in. Frank just stood there until Jim turned around and waved him to a seat. While he continued to talk on the phone, he pointedly looked at his watch. Frank took another deep breath and sat down, trying to keep a neutral expression on his face. Jim finished his conversation and put down the receiver.

"Frank, I wanted to speak to you about the Dawson project," he started. Frank cringed inwardly. He had just put the Dawson project on hold. He knew that it was the CEO's pet project to develop a new product to test in the market, but there were just no resources to work on it.

"I understand that you put the project on hold. Why?"

"Well," Frank started, attempting to gather his thoughts. "We just don't have the resources to work on it right now. We have a number of other prototypes for existing clients that we need to finish, and we just don't have the people to do it all."

"Be that as it may, Frank, the research on this new product concept indicates that it would help boost our market share considerably."

Frank could not disagree with that, and Jim's ideas for new products were usually right on target. But how could he get all the work done?

"Jim, I know how important this project is, but I have people working 50 or 60 hours a week, and important projects are still falling behind. I just have to have more resources to keep up."

"In our present economy, we can't do any more hiring. I think that maybe this is a question of organizing your people better to get things done. Frank, when I brought you into the VP Operations job, I felt that you had what it takes to do the job. Don't disappoint me now!"

Frank left Jim's office deep in thought. Jim just did not understand. He wanted things done and could not see what was happening. If only he could get some information out of the new project-tracking tool to show him what is really happening. With that thought, he headed down to Perry Smith's area to see what was happening on the Bigelow project.

Frank got back to his office around 5:30 P.M. His day had been a blur of meetings, consultations, and questions. He felt as if he had done nothing but solve everyone's problems except his own. As he entered his office, he could see the telephone light still flashing. Frank groaned. Amanda Stevens! He quickly dialed Amanda's number but only got her voice mail. He returned to his e-mail. The last e-mail in the list was from Amanda Stevens, and the title line was "About Your Promised Phone Call."

Frank muttered an expletive and shouted, "That's it!" to an empty office. "People around here have to start learning how to get things done."

He left a voice mail for his assistant to contact the project management consultant he had spoken to several weeks before. Several days later, Frank had an appointment with Greg Hughes, the consultant he had recently met. Greg was white-haired and a bit grizzled, evidence that he had been around the block managing projects over the years. Frank was back from another one of his interminable meetings when he received a call on his cell phone from reception that Greg was there. Frank stopped by reception and escorted Greg to his office.

"Sorry I'm late, Greg," Frank started. "I seem to be on a treadmill going backwards these days."

"Apology accepted," Greg answered. "I understand that things can get pretty busy."

After a few minutes of small talk, Greg said, "Frank, tell me what you think the problem is here."

"I really don't think that our people know how to manage projects. It seems like everything that we are trying to get done is either late, costing us a bunch of money because of mistakes, or just sitting still in the water. My people understand what must be done, they know when things are due, yet they still can't get things done. I spend all my time either getting on their backs to move things along or placating our clients. All I hear from my people is a bunch of excuses about why they can't perform. I even hired more staff and that didn't help. I really think that we need to train them all up on project management. What kind of course do you folks give?"

"Well, before we talk about training, could I ask a couple more questions?"

"Sure," Frank replied.

"You've told me a little about your problem, but could you tell me more about *why* you feel that training is the solution?"

"It seems like nobody knows how to get anything done. For example," Frank was thinking about the Deakins prototype, "we have to get a prototype out the door, and we know that the client is waiting on it. I go down to see them and they tell me, 'We'll be done in five days'. Five days later, it's another five days and another after that. They never get finished until our clients are hopping mad."

"Another example," said Frank, thinking of the Jones project, "is getting things done properly. I get a lot of complaints from our clients that we can't seem to get things done correctly, so we are forever making changes, long past when things ought to be done. It seems like every time we get it right, they change their minds about something or want us to do something more. Then they get on our backs because of their changes." Frank thought without pleasure about his last conversation with Amanda Stevens.

"We don't even seem to talk to each other," Frank added. "We have two projects for a client that are very similar, but our estimates to get them done were so different that the client was all over us. They really thought we were trying to cheat them. It took a lot of fast dancing to save those contracts."

Greg pondered what he had heard. "Could I ask you a couple more questions?" he asked. "I just want to be sure that I have a pretty good understanding of what you feel the problem is."

"Okay," said Frank, but he wondered, "How many questions does he need to ask in order to give us some training?"

"First of all, is this something new, or has it been going on for a while?"

"For as long as I can remember," Frank replied. "I have been in this position for four years now, and it's always been the same."

"How have other people reacted to the situation?"

"The CEO thinks I need to organize my people better. I'm not sure that he understands what I'm up against. My people certainly know there's a problem. I tell them all the time. But nothing ever changes," Frank added.

"Do you really want things to be different?" Greg asked.

"Absolutely! I don't know how much more of this I can take."

"Well, Frank, I don't feel that the answer to your problem is training, or at least training by itself," Greg started.

"Not training?" Frank interrupted him.

"At least, not training all by itself, and not just for the people managing projects," Greg continued.

"Well, if it's not training, what is it?" demanded Frank.

"Before we get to a possible solution, can I talk a bit more about the problem? This might take a few more minutes."

"As long as you're here already, I might as well listen."

"Great. Here is what I believe," Greg continued. "Albert Einstein once said 'You can't solve a problem with the same mind that created the problem.'[1] What he meant was when you have a problem, you must change your point of view or approach in order to find the solution. The same thinking that got you into the problem will not get you out. As I listen to you, I'm thinking of any number of occasions when I have met with a CEO, CIO, vice president of operations, or general manager, and I've heard your story, just with the details changed.

Here is the general story that I hear. If you could imagine the players speaking here, we might hear something like this:

- An executive like yourself says: 'We have a business to run here. I am telling people what I expect and what they need to get done, but it just does not happen.' And you are right!

- A manager person says: 'We are trying to get things done, but there is just too much happening, and we don't have the resources to cover it all!' And they are right, too.

- Finally, an employee chimes in: 'I have all this to do on my job, and now they pile all this other project stuff on top. I don't have time to do all of this!' And guess what, they are also right!"

"This is all I hear, all day every day. How did you know?" Frank exclaimed.

"I have seen and heard this same scenario so many times." Greg continued. "But underneath it all, it is always the same problem. You see, there are three things necessary to change your situation here—knowledge, expertise, and process." (See Exhibit 1.1.)

"*Knowledge* is information about a business and about the problem(s) the business may be suffering. Frank, you've told me a couple of things about your business and your problems, but at this point I don't know enough about the whole situation and in particular the root cause of your problem. When I talk about knowledge, I'm talking about more in-depth knowledge of what your business does and why the problems are happening. That will take some work, talking to people and analyzing your present situation and processes.

"*Expertise* is a different kind of knowledge; really, it's about what you do in a technical way. For example, your company is a manufacturer, so expertise for your area would involve knowledge about manufacturing in general, as well as about several different more specific things. New product development would also be expertise, as well as knowledge about widget manufacturing, inventory, and other topics that directly affect you. The important question here is, 'Where is the gap?' Is part of your problem that you lack expertise in some area?

"*Process* is really about how you do things. Let's take your new product development process. When you are developing a new product, you are applying your expertise in widgets to develop your new product. You are also going through a new product development process, first developing the idea, then prototyping, then testing. The question here is, 'Is there a problem in how you develop new products?' If you have a product that is late in delivery, we would want to get to the root of the problem. Is it because of a problem in your business? For example, are there too many new products being developed for your resources to handle? Or is it because you lack some expertise in a new type of widget design? Or is it because your new product development process lacks the step to get a clear idea of what the client wants the new widget to do, and so you must constantly re-do?

"I mentioned above an executive, a manager, and an employee. Any solution has to address all three people, or rather, all three levels of the business, in order to be successful. You really have to 'think strategically, plan tactically, and act operationally' in order to succeed. We call this strategic project management.

"Before we could recommend a solution, we must really understand what the problem is in all three of these areas. If project management is part of the root cause, then we can address that. The answer may not be just project management training, but I feel that it is worth the effort to find out what is really happening." Greg concluded.

"Well, I'm not really convinced yet, but I want to hear more."

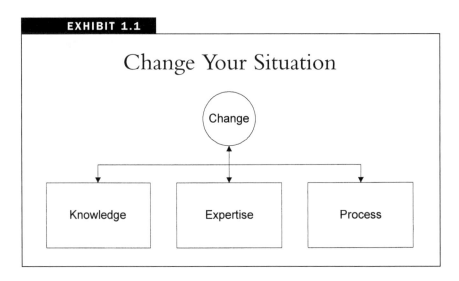

EXHIBIT 1.1

Change Your Situation

Change

Knowledge   Expertise   Process

"Okay, let's make an appointment to get into this in more detail and see how we can apply strategic project management to your situation."

"Let's do it!" Frank exclaimed.

The Real Problem

You may be asking yourself right about now how the story of your company wound up in this book. Not to worry, this story is not about just one company. You may also be asking the question, "What is the real problem here?" Greg Hughes first described the problem when he spoke about an executive, a manager, and an employee. Is the problem that people just don't know how to manage problems? No. That may be a part of the problem, but not the root of the problem. The real problem is found in the fundamental structure and manner of operations of many companies. In order to better illustrate the problem, let's look at the STO model (see Exhibit 1.2).

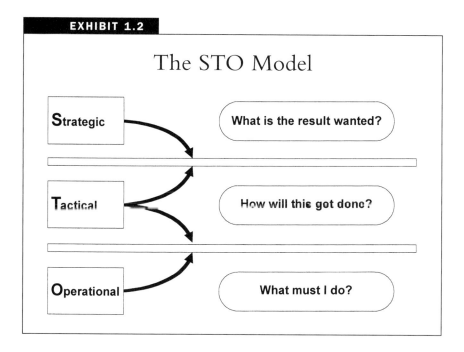

EXHIBIT 1.2

The STO Model

Strategic — What is the result wanted?

Tactical — How will this get done?

Operational — What must I do?

The STO Model

The STO model stands for "strategic, tactical, and operational" and shows the three levels of a company: the strategic/executive, the tactical/management, and the operational/employee. Each level contributes to a company in a different way. The STO model illustrates what each level's concerns are, as well as the root cause of the problem.

The strategic person asks the question, "What result do we want?" He or she is concerned with how to improve productivity and profitability, increase company value and return on investment. The concerns at this level are not tactical. They are not about how things will be done; they are about what needs to be done to make the company successful. As the situation relates to project management, there is often little or no input between the strategic and the tactical, because the strategic considers project management to be a tactical problem. It is as if a brick wall is constructed between the two levels. In the STO model, the solid black lines represent the brick wall and the arrows are the communications that don't get past the wall. So, from Frank Coleman's point of view, we hear, "I have a business to run here. I am telling people what I expect to get done, but it just does not happen."

The tactical person is asking, "How will we get this done?" He or she is generally concerned with how to achieve the priorities as envisioned by the executive, with the resources at hand. If all project decisions are made at the tactical level, then there is no oversight from a group that has a global vision of the company. In some companies, the brick wall may contain tiny holes here and there, so that a single manager can make a case for his or her projects. When this happens, the manager who was the last one to squeeze through the hole winds up with the highest project priority and the resources. That's why we hear Bob Jenkins, the project manager, saying: "We are trying to make changes, but there is just too much happening, and we don't have the resources to cover it all."

The operational person is concerned with, "What must I do?" These people actually get the work of the project done. They are concerned about how they will get their regular job done and do all of the project work besides. In many companies, employees are often assigned to projects in addition to their regular work. Employees often wind up feeling overworked and stressed in this situation. In the story of ABC Corp., we can almost hear the employees chime in: "We have our jobs to do, and now they pile all this stuff on top. We don't have time for all of this!"

The frustration described above is the result when lines of communication between the strategic (executive), the tactical (management), and the operational (employee) are not open.

The Purpose of This Book

Frank Coleman, the main character in the short story, is not a real person—at least not a single real person. He is a compilation of many people with whom we have worked over the years. After a while, you begin to see a recurring pattern of problems in companies that are challenged about the way they do things. The companies and situations change, but the underlying problems are the same. The challenges they face around project management always come down to a question of knowledge, expertise, and process. The authors of this book have experienced many of these situations and want to pass on some of the wisdom gleaned from these situations.

Large and complex projects are very difficult, it goes without saying. At times, it may seem as if small, simple projects act like large and complex projects. No matter what the project, the underlying principles of project management remain the same. When applied properly, the knowledge, tools, and techniques of project management can help your company become more productive and better at "getting things done."

The primary objective of this book is to show you what the basics of project management are so that you can begin making decisions and moving forward using project management in your company. When you finish this book, you will understand the fundamental principles, tools, and techniques of project management and how they can fit into the strategic thinking of your firm and help you achieve your business objectives. You will also see how strategic thinking can be linked to the tactical and operational levels, so that your projects will be aligned to your business objectives. When used properly, strategic project management can help your company become more efficient and profitable. This book will show you why that is so and how it can be done within your company.

How To Use This Book

In the opening story, Frank Coleman considered using a consultant to begin solving his problems. We would like you to consider this book as your first project management consultant. Although each chapter is self-contained and can be read on its own, we encourage you to read the book through completely to get the most out of it. You can always go back and concentrate on one chapter or another in order to consider your particular challenges.

Before going on, let's define several terms that are used frequently:

- *Project tool.* A project tool is a template, checklist, or other instrument used to carry out a project activity. Examples of tools would be a project charter checklist, a template for status reporting, or a template for a work breakdown structure. The word *tool* does *not* refer to software programs such as Microsoft Project® or Primavera®.

- *Project technique.* A project technique is a process employed to complete a project activity. For example, "decomposition" is the technique for creating a work breakdown structure, and "bottom-up estimating" is a technique for estimating project costs.

Although project management is a strategic tool, it must also be practical. We will show you how to decide which project management tools and techniques are appropriate for your circumstances and give you ideas about how to customize the tools to your needs. We will provide you with examples and templates for tools and techniques that you may wish to employ. You will find some examples of these tools and techniques in the text, and all of them are listed on the Web site (*www.wiley.com/go/pm*) that accompanies the book.

Each chapter of this book takes up a single subject area of project management and can be read on its own. There is a natural progression within the book; we cover project management in the same order that it normally functions. For example, we cover planning before we cover execution. We also discuss several other important subjects, such as

TIPS & TECHNIQUES

Project Tools versus Project Techniques

Project Tools

A template, checklist, or other instrument that is used to carry out a project activity. Examples of tools would be a project charter checklist, a template for status reporting, or a template for a work breakdown structure. Project tools are not necessarily software programs.

Project Techniques

A process employed to complete a project activity. For example, "decomposition" is the technique for creating a work breakdown structure, and "bottom-up estimating" is a technique for estimating project costs.

program management, the project management office, and project portfolio management, so that you understand what these other subjects are about and how project management relates to them.

There are brief case studies: examples about the actual challenges that other companies have faced. These stories are true, but the actual participants remain anonymous. Project success stories are also featured in the "In the Real World" examples to help you understand how different tools and techniques can be used effectively in different industries.

Another important element used throughout the book is called "Tips and Techniques." These sections contain practical information that you and other members of your organization can use right away.

Summary

Frank Coleman's story highlights the problems that are facing many companies today: resources that are stretched thin trying to complete too many poorly defined projects in too little time. The results are many projects that are late, over budget, and not delivering what is intended.

We have seen that the keys to solving these problems are knowledge about the company and the problem, the expertise to solve the problems, and a process with which to create solutions. The process, of course, is project management. We have also learned that project tools are templates, checklists, and other documents, not necessarily software products, and that project techniques are the processes used to carry out a project.

We hope that you enjoy reading this book and that it helps you and your company on your way toward becoming more efficient and profitable—a company that really knows how to "get things done."

Endnote

1. Albert Einstein citation obtained from: *http://www.therightside. demon.co.uk/quotes/einstein/*

CHAPTER 2

The Basics of Project Management

After reading this chapter you will be able to

- Understand the difference between projects and operations
- Understand what strategic project management is and why you should care about it
- Use the STO solution model to solve problems

What Is a Project?

Before we begin to discuss strategic project management, let's take a moment to identify what a project is and is not. According to the Project Management Institute, "A project is a temporary endeavor undertaken to create a unique product or service."[1] Harold Kerzner, a leading authority on project management says, "A project can be considered to be any series of activities and tasks that:

- Have a specific objective to be completed within certain specifications
- Have defined start and end dates
- Have funding limits (if applicable)
- Consume resources (i.e., money, people, equipment)"[2]

James P. Lewis, another leading authority, defines a project as "a one-time job that has defined starting and ending dates, a clearly specified objective, or scope to be performed, a pre-defined budget, and usually a temporary organization that is dismantled once the project is complete."[3]

Although each of these definitions has varying levels of detail, all agree on three important characteristics of projects. They are temporary, unique, and have a well-defined scope.

Let's look at the temporary characteristic of projects. The first characteristic of a project is that it should have a beginning and an end. Unfortunately, in today's ever-changing business world, some projects seem to appear mysteriously from within the depths of the organization and go on forever—without an end in sight. When asked about the origination of such projects, no one is really sure how the project was started or what the business goal was, often because members of the original team are no longer around and there is no archived history or documentation about the project. Also, the organization may not be quite sure how to end the project because it is not quite sure of the ramifications of doing so. A key question to ask for these Catch-22 projects is, "Has this project become, or always been, a part of ongoing operations?" Operations represent the daily functions of business; they follow the business cycle but never really end.

The second characteristic of a project is that the final deliverable is unique. For example, a manufacturer's process for developing a new product should be consistent and repeatable. Reinventing this process each time a new product needs to be developed would be costly and inefficient. However, this does not mean that the end deliverable will not have similarities with other deliverables. At the same time, each time the manufacturer goes through the process, it should be producing a product that is different in some way, shape, or form than other previous products. If not, then it is performing production in a costly and inefficient manner.

The third characteristic of a project is a defined scope. Defined scope means that the project is supposed to achieve a specific deliverable with

TIPS & TECHNIQUES

Definitions and Examples of Operations and Projects

Definitions

Operations:

- Ongoing
- Repetitive
- Produces the same thing

Project:

- Defined beginning and ending
- Unique deliverable
- Defined scope

Examples of ongoing operations

- Factory production of products
- Completing a payroll run
- Accounts Payable and Receivable

Examples of a project with a defined beginning and end

- Designing a new product
- Installing a new software system to do payroll
- Redesigning a new Accounts Payable process

specific attributes at the end of the project. Although this sounds simple, challenges arise when defining project scope, which we will go into detail about in Chapter 4. However, the key thing to remember about scope is to be sure that one exists. There are three components of a project that typically determine scope: time, cost, and quality. Laurence J. Peter, an American educator, once said, "If you don't know where you are going, you will probably end up somewhere else."[4] Mr. Peter was not a project manager, but he had the right idea. Without defining the scope of your project, it is very difficult to know where you will end up. Even well-planned projects sometimes fall prey to *scope creep*; that is, the end deliverable continues to grow and change without control and the project usually finishes over budget and late.

A well-defined scope is also the foundation of a project budget. If you do not know what you are creating, it is impossible to know how much it will cost.

What Is Project Management?

Now that we have an idea of what a project is, let's return to our expert sources for definitions of project management. The Project Management Institute defines project management as "the application of knowledge, skills, tools and techniques to project activities to meet project requirements."[5] Harold Kerzner expands on this, saying:

> Project Management is the planning, organizing, directing, and controlling of company resources for a relatively short-term objective that has been established to complete specific goals and objectives. Furthermore, project management utilizes the systems approach to management by having functional personnel (the vertical hierarchy) assigned to a specific project (the horizontal hierarchy).[6]

Finally, according to James P. Lewis, "Project Management is the planning, scheduling, and controlling of project activities to achieve project objectives."[7]

These definitions of project management, like the definitions of a project, highlight certain characteristics that are important to project management. The most important characteristic of project management is that it is oriented toward achieving results. The whole purpose of project management is to accomplish the business result that is desired. We emphasize this point here for a reason—project management is not an end in itself; it is a process to achieve an end. For an organization that is implementing project management, it is often difficult to see the forest through the trees.

Today's marketplace has many methodologies, strategies, tools, and consultants to help an organization implement project management. We believe that the minimal approach is the best, and less is more. In other words, an organization should implement only those project processes, tools, and techniques that are necessary to achieve success in its projects and environment. To do any more will not only be costly but may also be counterproductive to the desired organizational impact.

Finally, let's look at the definition of strategic project management: "Strategic Project Management is the use of the appropriate project management knowledge, skills, tools, and techniques in the context of the company's goals and objectives, so that the project deliverables will contribute to company value in a way that can be measured."[8]

Management of projects must be aligned with the mission, goals, and objectives of a company so that the projects move the company recognizably closer to achieving its business results.

TIPS & TECHNIQUES

What Is Project Management?

Project Management is the planning, scheduling, and controlling of project activities to achieve project objectives.[a]

a. James P. Lewis, *The Project Manager's Desk Reference* (New York: McGraw-Hill, 1995).

TIPS & TECHNIQUES

What is Strategic Project Management?

Strategic Project Management is the use of the appropriate project management knowledge, skills, tools, and techniques in the context of the company's goals and objectives, so that the project deliverables will contribute to company value in a way that can be measured.

Some practitioners of project management might interject at this point, saying that good project management should automatically take this into account through correct project processes. They would not be incorrect in saying so; however, our experience shows that in many companies, strategic project management does not exist at all. Instead, project management is seen as a process to be used at the tactical or operation level, and not an executive's concern. This is a crucial, erroneous assumption, and the evidence that the assumption is made is constantly all around us.

The Real Problem and Project Management

In the last chapter, we introduced the STO model to illustrate the problem with project management. If we take a closer look at the STO model, we can begin to discern the problems that exist in some organizations. If you look at the model, the thick black line between each level represents a barrier, a "brick wall" if you will, that blocks proper project communication between levels. In many organizations, the brick wall between the strategic and tactical levels is caused by the tendency of many executives to consider project management more like a toolkit, something for the managers at the tactical level to worry about. In the Real World, "Imposition from Above" illustrates this point quite effectively.

This story illustrates a very important point: some projects are technically considered a success. That is, they come in on time, on budget, and within scope. However, as illustrated, they do not actually deliver what the business needs, and so they are not only of little use, but they also cost the organization time, money, and wasted resources. Why does

IN THE REAL WORLD

Imposition from Above

The executives of a services company with about 30,000 employees that had about one-third of their employees working on projects at any given time decided that something needed to be done about tracking internal and client projects. A large portion of the organization's budget was for project work, yet they did not feel that they understood how that money was being spent and what the projects were returning to the company's bottom line. It seemed to them that many of the projects were not necessary, but it was difficult to discern just what the problem was, given the lack of information available. The problem was, they felt that significant resources were being spent with no real accountability.

The executives mandated that a project team be formed in the Information Technology department to decide on an appropriate tool to implement. After analyzing a series of technical solutions, the project team proposed one solution to the executives, and they were given the mandate to proceed with implementation. The project team decided to implement an online solution because of their geographic challenge, which often required distributed project teams with members on three continents. The tool they chose could be accessed through the company intranet or through the Internet, for international locations. Satisfied that they had chosen the best solution, the funds were approved and the project commenced.

IN THE REAL WORLD CONTINUED

This actual project was finished on time and within the proposed budget, so it could be dubbed a success, right?

Wrong! As difficult as it is to believe, neither the executives nor the project team ever consulted with management (tactical) to discover what the root problem was.

The assumption was made that the business problem was one of tracking and communications and that the chosen deliverable would solve the problem. No consideration was ever given to management and operational processes. Remember the three components of scope—time, cost, and performance? This project met all three objectives, but when it was put into operation, the tool wound up providing useless information at a very high cost.

What went wrong? In this case, a lack of communication between the executive group that sponsored and approved the project and the managers and project managers who would use the end product proved to be the crucial missing link. The operational people who were supposed to use the tool did not understand how to use it. The information they were required to input into the system did not mesh with the information their project processes produced, and the format was at such a high level of detail that the resulting reports were meaningless.

This case is an example of what can happen when the brick wall is in place between the strategic and tactical levels of the organization. The business objective of the project—to improve the decision-making information at the executive level—was a valid objective for the project and supported the business mission and objectives. However, the project did not take into account *all* of the people who would be affected by the project, nor the context that the project was taking place in (i.e., the existing project management processes and project structure). As a result, a "successful" project actually failed.

this happen? In order to understand, let's take a closer look at why projects are initiated in the first place.

A project usually is conceived to solve a problem or make a change. For example, a product that a company produces may be at the mature end of its life cycle in the marketplace. The company knows that it must be replaced with another product at some point in time in order to maintain or increase market share and keep revenues flowing. The process of developing a new product is a project. It solves a problem (i.e., how to keep market share and revenues flowing).

Problems also occur when there is a lack of communication from the tactical level to the strategic level. Think of that brick wall; it blocks upward communication as well as downward communication.

Sometimes projects are started as the pet idea of a person within the company. Other projects may be conceived to address an internal problem, such as the second story or because a firm is growing rapidly and finds that manual processes and software spreadsheets are no longer adequate to perform human resources functions properly. Finding the solution to their problem will also become a project.

We can categorize business problems in many different ways: IS/IT, process and production, time-to-market, carrying costs, productivity, profitability, integration, inventory, and many more. At a fundamental level, problems could be identified as reduced profits, reduced company value, and smaller market share. To correct any of these problems, something must change. Remember what Albert Einstein once said, "You can't solve a problem with the same mind that made it." In other words, to solve a problem, you must find new information or a new perspective to consider.

In order to solve a problem, you must know several things: what the problem is, what the root cause of the problem is, what the solution is, and most important, how to make the solution work. That sounds really simple, but experience shows that it is not easy. Let's look at the

TIPS & TECHNIQUES

Getting a Grip on Project Management

Ask yourself the following questions:

Q: Do you resemble Frank Coleman from Chapter 1 even a little bit?

A:

Q: Are you overwhelmed by all of the work that must be accomplished?

A:

Q: Do there seem to be more projects than people or resources to do them?

A:

Q: What are your company's top three business goals?

A:

Q: Are all of your projects aligned with these goals? If not, why not?

A:

Q: What are the business results you want to achieve this quarter?

A:

three areas to consider when solving a problem: knowledge, expertise, and process.

Knowledge is information about a business and about the problem(s) the business may be experiencing. A very popular manner of problem solving in American business today could best be described as Fire, Aim, Ready! A problem is found, and without much analysis, a solution is put in place. Often, the ramifications of the solution are only known after the solution is in place; the fix is often worse than the original problem. This type of problem solving happens everywhere. On a production line, a quick fix can cause havoc farther down the line. A quick fix to a programming bug can crash the whole system. Knowledge in this context is the careful consideration of all aspects of the problem, including the technical and business context in which the problem is found and the root cause analysis that will help prevent the problem from occurring again.

Expertise is topical or technical knowledge that addresses a specific area of undertaking with the intent of finding a solution. Examples of expertise are systems development, supply chain management, customer relationship management (CRM) systems, or quality. A business must ask itself whether it has the expertise in-house to effectively implement a solution to the problem. If the company does not have the expertise internally, it must look for outside help.

TIPS & TECHNIQUES

Before implementing a solution, ask yourself the following questions:

Q: How will the solution to this problem affect other areas of the business?

A:

Q: How will the solution affect the customer, the supplier, and every other entity involved?

A:

Q: Does the business have the proper perspective to properly identify the solution? At times, an outside perspective may be needed to help determine the real cause of the problem.

A:

Process is defined as the tools and methodologies that are required to actually create change to solve the problem. A recent study published by the Project Management Institute[9] highlights a "knowing-doing" gap that is prevalent in businesses today. The study points out that many businesses seem to know what needs to be done, but they are not able to execute a strategy to create change. The process necessary to get things done is the STO solution model.

As referenced earlier in this chapter, the Project Management Institute defines project management as "the application of knowledge, skills, tools and techniques to project activities to meet project requirements." As you will recall, our definition emphasizes the word *strategic*, meaning that we apply these processes at a strategic level within a business, using the appropriate project management knowledge, skills, tools, and techniques in the context of the company's goals and objectives, so that the project deliverables will contribute to company value in ways that can be measured. Strategic project management is a process that takes into account a company's way of doing business, allowing for the possibility of a significant payoff with fewer risks. It can propel companies to better achieve corporate goals.

For example, a company wanted to reduce turnover of its operations staff. Understanding the importance of this project, a vice president of the organization worked with a group to define the scope of the project and the characteristics that would be used to measure the results. The solution for this project included the following deliverables:

- Complete job analysis of the various roles in the field organization
- Core competencies for associates and their managers
- A behavioral-based interviewing program based on the new job profiles, descriptions, and competencies
- Analysis of the compensation structure for this group

- Train-the-trainer for management

One year later, the efforts resulted in about a 10 percent reduction in turnover for the organization. The point here is that working closely with executive leadership to determine all of the possible issues that would affect the performance of those associates made the difference.

Now that we understand what strategic project management is and why you should care about it, let's focus on the STO perspective.

The STO Solution Model

Now that we have seen how the STO perspective explains the real problem, let's take a look at how the STO solution model can help solve the real problem. The STO solution model includes not only the three perspective levels within the company—strategic, tactical, and operational—but also the five project management processes: initiation, planning, execution, control, and closing. When the levels and the project management processes are properly aligned, the firm is able to "think strategically, plan tactically, and act operationally." The real key to success is proper communication across the levels. When the brick walls are torn down and communications lines are installed, projects can truly be aligned with the company's mission, goals, and objectives (see Exhibit 2.1).

Before we explain how this model works, let's briefly describe each of the project management processes. In subsequent chapters, each of these processes is explained in more detail. This is just an introduction so that we may further explore the crucial relation between project management and the STO model.

Project Initiation

The book *A Guide to the Project Management Body of Knowledge* defines project initiation as "the process of formally authorizing a new project

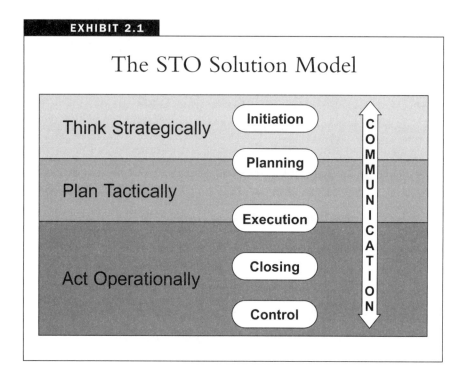

EXHIBIT 2.1

The STO Solution Model

Think Strategically — Initiation

Planning

Plan Tactically

Execution

Closing

Act Operationally

Control

COMMUNICATION

or that an existing project should continue into its next phase."[10] During project initiation, the company or organization officially recognizes that there is a project. This is really the first stab at what the project is about. In some cases, different types of project feasibility studies have already been done before the project is initiated. If they have not been done, now is when they should start. At this early stage of a project, it is most important to understand the business need the project will address. How will this project really contribute to company value? Another important end of project initiation is to create a preliminary definition of what the project will deliver: Is it a product or a service? What are its characteristics and attributes? Not having the high-level deliverables defined at this point often leads to scope creep. In the Real World, "Aligning Projects with Business Strategy" illustrates how to focus on the real business need when initiating a project.

Project initiation is also the time when the organization commits to the project. It may not be a final commitment (that may occur after detailed planning is done), but an initial commitment of time and resources, along with an indication of whether sufficient resources will be available to carry out the project to its end. It is also important at this stage to begin to identify the stakeholders, the people the project will affect in any way. Finally, during project initiation, the project manager is identified.

IN THE REAL WORLD

Aligning Projects with Business Strategy

One of the most important concepts in project management is the alignment of projects with business strategy. *Bottom line*: Any project that does not support business strategy should not be executed.

Hewitt Associates, Inc. demonstrated the link between strategy and projects when it implemented an employee performance management system recently. It is often difficult to establish such a link in a project that supports internal processes. However, by incorporating support for business strategy into the new system, Hewitt clearly made the connection.

Hewitt had undergone rapid expansion during the second half of the 1990s, partly because of an expansion of business activities from its original base, with benefits outsourcing a particular area of growth. To ensure continued strong performance among a growing number of new associates, Hewitt had instituted a new 360-degree assessment process. Each associate's performance was assessed by 6 to 12 people, including peers, direct reports, managers, and even clients. At the time, the several thousand managers in the company were often spending 30 to 40 hours, twice a year, creating and e-mailing assessment documents and then many more hours consolidating the returned feedback—not an insignificant drag on productivity. Plus, the feedback requested was often not related to the associate's performance goals, making evaluation of the associate's success in meeting those goals very difficult.

During initiation of the performance management project, the project team and the sponsor determined how they could move company objectives forward. Their goals for the project were as follows:

- Connect associate performance and development goals, coaching, and performance assessment to focus associate work and learning on firm objectives.

- Automate processes to free up manager and associate time to do that work.

To meet these goals, Hewitt developed a competency-based system to guide the entire performance cycle. The competencies defined the skills required to meet the goals of each role, which in turn supported business objectives. With clearly defined competencies and goals, associates could see how they fit into the Hewitt picture and choose appropriate activities for work today and for developing their skills for future work.

The project team next considered a make-or-buy decision. When they found no software that could accommodate multiple sets of competencies and streamline the performance management processes without a great deal of software customization, the team decided to create the software.

The resulting system allowed associates to document performance and development plans, including specific goals for developing the competencies required for their roles. Coaching and feedback throughout the performance year were to focus on associates' success in moving toward accomplishment of their goals. Managers used the performance and development plans at the end of the year to create feedback requests, and assessors in turn provided the needed feedback on how well associates met their goals.

When the new system was implemented, the immediate response was so positive that management rolled out the system to the entire firm immediately, rather than wait six months. Fortunately, the team developed the system to be scalable from the start. At the end of the first year of use, the new system had a utilization rate of more than 80 percent, and managers were thrilled with the time saved. Many managers and administrators were able to achieve better than 50 percent time savings using the new system.

By carefully considering how the project could support the overall strategy of the company, Hewitt Associates was able to have a major impact on associate development and productivity for an investment that was quite modest compared to the payoff.

Project Planning

Project planning or, more properly, the project planning process consists of a series of essential and supporting processes whose outcome is a project plan that can then be executed. After initiation, the process of project planning is the most important phase of project management. After project initiation, it is also the most ignored phase of project management. During project planning, the project team will flesh out the details of the high-level deliverables and develop the work tasks that must be done to create them. During the planning process, the aspects of planning that are addressed are as follows:

- Quality
- Risk
- Communications
- Organization
- Procurement

The project planning deliverable (sometimes called a "project book") consists of the analysis of the high-level deliverables (often referred to as a work breakdown structure), the set of tasks that must be completed, a project schedule, budget, and plans to deal with quality, risk, communications, resources, and procurement. This set of documents becomes the basis for project execution.

Project Execution and Controlling

Although these are two separate processes, they happen together. In addition, these two processes are much less complex to explain; however, being simpler does not mean easier. Project execution is nothing more than performing all of the work as it is detailed in the project plan. If planning has been done well, project execution and control will be accomplished with fewer problems. Some of the crucial aspects of project execution include gathering and disseminating information; soliciting, contracting, and administering vendor contracts; and developing the project team and quality assurance. Gathering information on a regular basis is important to understand how the project is progressing. Often, problems that may occur to delay a project happen in the first

TIPS & TECHNIQUES

Getting Back on Track

Ask yourself the following questions:

Q: If, after you are finished with only 15 percent of a project, you are already 5 percent behind, how will you get back on track?

A:

Q: What about a 35 percent delay?

A:

few weeks of a project. By gathering information and analyzing it right away, you can catch these problems before they become major.

Think about the questions in Tips and Techniques, "Getting Back on Track." Because the estimated resources were not able to complete the work on time, more effort must be expended beyond what was originally planned. Where will this effort come from? If you do not gather information early enough, and you wait until the project is advanced, say 30 percent or 40 percent, even more effort will have to be expended because the increased time passed by will almost certainly increase the delay. If a 15 percent delay was going to be difficult to overcome, how about a 35 percent delay? Gather the information early and regularly, so that corrective action can be taken as soon as possible. A last note on gathering information: As you gather more detailed information about your projects, you begin to build an important source of knowledge for future projects. Understanding, for example, how long certain tasks actually took, in comparison with the estimated time, can be an important resource for future planning.

Controlling processes is like keeping your finger on the pulse. Each of these processes—scope verification and control, schedule control, quality control, cost control, and risk monitoring and control—provide information about the health of your project. All of them are important, often in combination, to diagnosing any problems. Scope controls are about your actual deliverables. They ask the questions, "Is all of the deliverable there?" and "Is only the deliverable there?" As we mentioned earlier, scope creep often becomes scope gallop. Keeping an eye on what is being delivered can help keep the horse in the corral. Cost control and schedule control must often be considered together in order to really understand what is happening inside of a project. Here's an example: Looking at the schedule, you see that a project is coming in below cost. That seems like good news. If you walk away and don't ask more questions, you won't have the whole picture. If the cost is below budget because delays have kept some resources from starting their work, you may be below now, but farther down the road, when the resources must work overtime to get their work done on time, you risk not only being late but also over cost in the long run.

Quality assurance, a process from project execution, and quality control are often confused. Probably the best way of looking at them is like this:

- Quality assurance is making sure that your project tasks and activities are being carried out in accordance with the project plan and specifications. If you do, you will reduce your chances of having problems with quality later on.

- Quality control is asking the question, "Does this deliverable meet specifications, and does it perform as it is supposed to?"

Effort on the first makes the last a lot less demanding.

Finally, let's talk briefly about risk, which is usually paired with opportunity. There is always risk involved with any project. The role of a project manager in a project is to take those risks that have the most probability and the greatest impact on the project, identify what opportunities lie within those risks, and minimize the chance of risk occurring while maximizing any opportunities that may arise from risk.

Closing

Closing processes are used to mark the end of the project. If there is a client involved, these processes are primarily concerned with having the sponsor officially accept and sign off on the project deliverable. For external vendors, these processes may have legal ramifications related to payment of the contract. In the case of internal projects, closing is about gathering information about how the project went and lessons learned about what went right and wrong. Looking at the tasks and activities to see where you can improve in the future is valuable for your organization.

When you have tracked a sufficient number of projects, you can then use these lessons learned to develop best practices and project templates, both of which make planning much easier for future projects.

The Five Project Processes and the STO Solution Model

Now that we have given a brief overview of each of the project processes, let's see how they fit into the STO solution model (see Exhibit 1.1).

Think Strategically

As mentioned before, initiation is the process of identifying that there are projects to be done, and assigning priorities relative to business mission, goals, and objectives. During initiation, the ultimate results of the project (deliverables) are defined. The project may be to solve a problem, design a new product for the market, increase sales, or implement a new information system, among others. The objective of the initiation process is to identify where the problem or need exists, what is its effect on business results, and how the business wants those results to change. In this way, the resulting projects will be aligned with the mission, goals, and objectives of the company.

If initiation is not done directly by executives, it must have input and approval from the executive level in order to be successful. Lack of executive input leads to a lack of planning around resources, conflicting priorities, and generally less successful projects. Results can cause a decrease in profits, products being late to market, or costly out-of-date information systems.

Plan Tactically

Planning begins at the strategic level and is driven down to the tactical level. Planning is determining at a greater level of detail what deliverables are necessary to complete the project and what resources (e.g., people, materials, time) will be needed to complete the project successfully. At the tactical and operational levels, planners may then determine the actual work to be done in the appropriate time and with what materials. Because the executive has provided guidance and made a commitment to project priorities, management may now actually assign the appropriate resources to the project, with the support of the executive.

Act Operationally

Execution is carrying out the various tasks that will produce the deliverables intended by the project. It begins at the tactical level, but proceeds mostly at the operational level. Control happens in parallel with execution at the operational level. It is the process of capturing appropriate information that will be compared to expected results in order to document project progress in a quantifiable way. During project closing, all deliverables are finalized and accepted by the executive, and lessons learned are documented for future reference.

Communications

The one key that ties this model together is communication. Communication is the transfer of information to the right people at the right time. At the operational level, a greater level of detail is required in order to keep project team members in sync. At the tactical level, the information is at a higher level, but it is still detailed enough to allow management to know what is going on. At the strategic level, only the most important information around project scope, time, and cost is to know that the project is achieving the results required. When there is a problem in execution, the executive level needs to know fast, not last.

Summary

In this chapter, we have defined a project as a series of tasks that have both a beginning and an end, a defined scope that culminates in a unique deliverable. Project management is the process to initiate, plan, execute, control, and close a project. We have introduced the STO (strategic, tactical, and operational) model and used it to illustrate the problems that many organizations have with project management. We have also used the STO model to illustrate the solution to those problems in terms of project management. Initiation, planning, execution, control, and closing are defined as follows:

- *Initiation*. The objective of initiation is to align these concerns with the actual projects to be done. The executive communicates the vision that drives initiation and planning in the right direction. The executive also communicates priorities to the tactical level. The results of initiation and planning in this manner are increased productivity, profitability, company value, and return on investment (ROI), as well as improved capability.

- *Planning*. Working with this information to plan the projects so that they will achieve the results increases productivity, improves profitability, and shows positive ROI, as well as achieving the priorities as envisioned by the executive.

- *Execution, control, and closing.* Uses the proper project processes to keep in alignment with the executive goals to produce the desired results. Also uses proper metrics to monitor actual results to compare with the goals.

In the next chapter, we take an in-depth look at the initiation process in the context of strategic project management.

Endnotes

1. *A Guide to the Project Management Body of Knowledge* (Newton Square, PA: Project Management Institute, 2000).

2. Harold Kerzner, Ph.D., *Project Management: A Systems Approach to Planning, Scheduling, and Controlling* (New York: John Wiley & Sons, 1998).

3. James P. Lewis, *The Project Manager's Desk Reference* (New York: McGraw-Hill, 1995).

4. Copyright 1994–2003, QuotationsPage.com and Michael Moncur. All rights reserved.

5. See note 1.

6. See note 2.

7. See note 3.

8. Kevin R. Callahan, "The STO Model," white paper (The Project Management Consortium, Inc., 2002).

9. Janice Thomas, Connie L. Delisle, Kam Jugdev, *Selling Project Management to Senior Executives* (Newton Square, PA: The Project Management Institute, 2002).

10. Ibid. There are many different project management methodologies around. We use *A Guide to the Project Management Body of Knowledge (PMBOK)* as our methodology; therefore, we quote most of our definitions from that source.

CHAPTER 3

Project Initiation

After reading this chapter you will be able to

- Determine your organization's type and how its structure may affect project management
- Connect business objectives with project objectives
- Define the difference between product life cycle and project life cycle
- Define project initiation and why it is important
- Identify the roles within project initiation
- Understand what a project charter is and how it is created

What Is Project Context?

Project management does not happen in a vacuum; many different factors can affect the success of a project. Among the most important factors is the organizational context. The way in which the organization functions, who has authority, and how decisions are made will all influence a project. Three types of organizations are discussed here, along with some variations of each type. The three basic organization types are functional, matrix, and projectized (see Exhibit 3.1). Project management will happen in different ways in each of these organizations, so a firm that wants to institute project management will need to understand what effect the organization structure will have and what obstacles and challenges will need to be overcome.

Functional Organization

The functional organization is a traditional company that has well-defined divisions and departments. Each division and department has a structured chain of authority that indicates, at least on paper, who is in charge of each group and has the authority to make decisions. Authority runs vertically, and there are definite gateways between different divisions. It

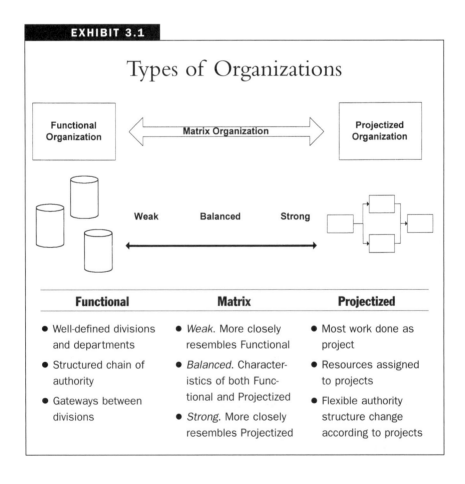

EXHIBIT 3.1

Types of Organizations

Functional	Matrix	Projectized
• Well-defined divisions and departments	• *Weak*. More closely resembles Functional	• Most work done as project
• Structured chain of authority	• *Balanced*. Characteristics of both Functional and Projectized	• Resources assigned to projects
• Gateways between divisions	• *Strong*. More closely resembles Projectized	• Flexible authority structure change according to projects

would not be unusual to find a certain amount of conflict about who has authority over a particular area. In many ways, the functional company can be compared to a group of silos within a silo. At times, it is very difficult to communicate among the silos. As a result, change is a big challenge in this type of organization.

Imagine a project to upgrade the customer relationship management system in a functional organization. At a minimum, the team would include representatives of several divisions or departments (e.g., sales, marketing, finance, and information technology). If these departments are not used to working together in this fashion, the project will have a rocky road to travel.

The project manager will not have any authority over any member of the team, and the team as a whole may not have the authority to make any major decisions. The project manager will be little more than a project coordinator or administrator (we will discuss these roles at length later in this chapter), and project paralysis occurs as risk decisions require extensive consultation outside of the team.

The person or group that is championing project management in this type of organization must understand the challenge being faced and properly prepare for implementing project management. This would include the support of the executive of the organization, which would be necessary to overcome the resistance of silos up and down the organization.

Projectized Organization

The projectized organization is at the other end of the spectrum from the functional organization. In a projectized organization, a significant portion of the organization's work is done in projects. As a result, structures are in place to promote project work. Many employees who do project work would not have a permanent assignment beyond their current project team. In place of the vertical structure of a functional organization, there would be a more flexible structure that would change as projects are begun, executed, and closed.

Often there are support personnel who would handle the project team member's needs, such as human resources, but the team member's manager is the project manager. Teams are made up of people who have expertise in the different areas as required by the project, and they are supported by centers of expertise, one of which would be project management.

In the projectized organization, the project manager actually has significant authority, not only over the team members but also over the projects. Achieving a projectized organization is difficult, which is why there are more functional and matrix organizations in this world.

Matrix Organization

Matrix organizations combine the characteristics of both functional and projectized organizations to varying degrees. Within the domain of matrix organizations are three classifications: strong, balanced, and weak. Each of these classifications denotes organizations that have varying degrees of the characteristics of both functional and projectized organizations.

The strong matrix organization more closely resembles the projectized organization. Many employees are involved in project work. Rather than being assigned to the project team permanently, many employees have homes in functional areas and are only lent to the project. An important aspect to note here is that there are few, if any, obligations on them from their functional area during the project. For the most part, they are focused on one or more projects at any given time.

Like the projectized organization, part of the role of the functional areas is to support project work. The most important aspect of the strong matrix organization is the function of project management. In this case, this is usually a separate functional area to which all project managers belong and from which they are assigned to projects. It is also important to note that the project manager would have significant authority in the strong matrix organization, although not as much as in the projectized organization.

The balanced matrix organization, as its name suggests, takes its characteristics almost equally from the projectized and functional organizations. The employees who staff projects come from different functions within the organization, including the project manager.

Usually, project management is not a separate function but expertise that is developed within a functional area. The project manager has less authority in this organization, but normally enough authority to run the team effectively. At times, for smaller projects, a project administrator may substitute for the project manager.

The weak matrix organization is much closer to the functional organization. Team members come from different functional areas, and they often continue working in their areas along with the project. The team has a project coordinator who does not have significant authority.

One of the biggest challenges to this structure is in helping team members find the time to do project work. Because they still report to the functional organization, they often have trouble finding time to do project work and see it as an extra burden rather than as part of their jobs. Because many weak matrix organizations still have their vertical structure, their managers are not very sympathetic with project needs. This situation calls for strong leadership from the project sponsor in order to succeed.

Other Project Management Influences

In addition to the organizational context, there are several other influences on project management, including industry type, the state of the economy, legal concerns, and others. There is often (although not always) a correlation between industry and organization type. For example,

What Structural Barriers Exist in Your Organization?

Q: What type of organizational structure do you have (i.e., Functional, Matrix, or Projectized)?

A:

Q: How does your structure hinder project management in your organization?

A:

Q: What discussions might you have with your leadership to become more project friendly?

A:

older manufacturing companies may tend more toward a functional organization than a projectized organization. Although there are projects to be done in a manufacturing company, it is more difficult to carry them out if they are functional.

For example, the pharmaceutical industry is highly regulated; new drug development has many rules and regulations to follow. Part of good project management in this industry is ensuring that all of these regulations are carried out. In newer service industries that are more intensively focused on customers, such as benefits outsourcing, the chances of finding a projectized company are much greater.

Breaking Down the Wall

Now that we have seen the context of project management as background, let's return to our discussion of the walls between the different levels of companies: the strategic (executive), the tactical (management), and the operational (employee). These walls are often the result of the type of organization, the industry, or just attitudes about project management.

For example, it is easy to see how in a functional organization, information is retained in a particular division. When the information does not circulate, a wall goes up. There are several reasons that this situation might exist, such as employees protecting turf or simply believing that the responsibility lies in their own divisions.

At other times, the wall is about control issues at the management level between different groups in the organization. We are not suggesting that these walls are built on purpose to harm the company; the opposite is actually true. However, the walls must come down in order to help the organization become more successful. What we can see clearly, though, is that certain types of organizations do not inherently facilitate project management.

Beyond organizational type, there are reasons that executives do not see project management from a strategic point of view. A recent study published by the Project Management Institute (PMI) found that "experiences indicated that Project Managers and Senior Executives do not realize the strategic value of Project Management beyond its role as a control mechanism."[1] In other words, in these cases, executives and project managers saw project management as a simple tool to be used to track a project, rather than as a strategic tool that can help an organization work more productively and more efficiently.

The research showed that executives still are more apt to turn to project management in a crisis, as opposed to a new way of working or seeking competitive advantages. Why does this type of attitude prevail? There are many reasons, and some of them are related to the development of project management as a profession.

One reason is that project management is placed in the domain of Information Technology. This is not surprising, because in many organizations today, that is the only place where project management occurs. However, project management has long been a very important profession in several industries such as construction, aviation, and defense. Despite this historical usage, project management is still developing as a separate profession in many industries. As a result, some confusion exists about what project management is and what its place is in an organization.

Another reason is that the project management life cycle is confused with the product (or service) development life cycle, and a project manager's role is confused with that of a technical or subject matter expert. Still another reason is that organizations acquire a project management tool of some sort (usually software), and many consider that to be implementing project management. It is a start, but only a start. In many other cases, executives do not see the strategic importance of project management, or for that matter, neither do many managers and project professionals. Breaking down the walls involves increasing information and changing those attitudes.

Change is never easy, and breaking down the walls in an organization's STO (strategic, tactical, operational) structure is a challenge. Making this type of change usually requires the sponsorship and change leadership of an executive or senior manager in the organization. Education around project management is important, and a short introductory seminar can be helpful. Reading books (such as this one!) can also be helpful in spreading the word about project management. Probably one of the most persuasive ways to raise the level of strategic project management is to achieve significant success with a project that contributes notably to the organization's success. Building coalitions around success, along with senior sponsorship, are among the best ways to promote project management and break down the wall.

The Benefits of Breaking Down the Wall

As the walls begin to break down, significant benefits will become evident, including better alignment of projects with organizational objectives. Organizations will discover whether they are focusing on what is important. A director of a major division in a Fortune 500 company put it well when he said, "When we began implementing project management in our department, we became aware of a number of stealth projects that we did not know about."

As an organization becomes more aware of which projects are important, it can begin to look at all of its projects to see which ones will benefit the organization (portfolio management) most, as well as begin to coordinate the resources necessary for each project in a rational manner (program management). The benefits then cascade down through the project processes. Planning becomes more reliable because the objectives and high-level deliverables it is based on are strategically aligned.

The Difference Between Project and Product Life Cycles

Here is a typical job posting for a project management position:

> Five plus years of project management experience. Three plus years of Documentum content management and workflow experience required. Experience with Web development and J2EE principles. Must have worked with the following platforms: Unix, Sybase, Documentum, BEA WebLogic or other J2EE application server. Experience with Sybase databases required. Ability to work in the following languages: Java, JSP, DocBasic, DQL. Experience with design tool: Documentum Developer Studio. Experience with MS Project.

Note that project management experience is barely included in the listing. What the listing goes into extensively are the technical requirements of the position and the ability to work with certain types of technology and particular programming languages. This is an example of confusing the role of project manager with that of what we call a technical team lead or subject matter expert.

We can be fairly certain that anyone being interviewed for the position would be posed this question, "Are you a hands-on project manager?" In other words, in the context of an Information Systems project, do you write code, troubleshoot individual bugs, and understand all of the configuration requirements of the database that is being used. Are you a technology expert? The right answer to this question is that if the project manager must start writing code and configuring software, the project is in trouble from the beginning. It is very difficult to both manage a project and work on individual project tasks at the same time.

A person who is trying to fulfill both the project manager role and the technology team lead role will have difficulty working at two levels. A project manager must keep the broad view of the project in focus, ensuring that all parts of the project are moving ahead as scheduled. The technical team lead will dive into the details of the project, assisting various team members and looking at the project with a very narrow view. It is nearly impossible to fulfill both of these roles at once.

Now, we are not saying that the project manager does not need any knowledge of the subject area that the project is addressing, or even that it is not good for the project manager to have worked intimately in the knowledge area of the project. We are saying that detailed expertise in the subject matter is not necessary for the professional project manager.

In order to explain, let's look at the example of a major construction project to build a 25-story office building. Here, the project manager is coordinating and tracking the activities of multiple subcontractors: the concrete company, the steel company, the construction workers, and others.

The project manager certainly must have a grasp of construction activities, but would we expect him or her to jump into the hole dug for the foundation and start pouring concrete or climb onto a steel beam and start riveting? Of course not! In any construction project where this happened, we would rightfully be concerned about the quality of the building, because the project manager can't grasp the overall picture when he or she is down in the foundation pouring concrete.

Yet on many other types of projects, that is exactly what is expected. If you refer back to the job requirements cited previously, you find that often there is no requirement regarding the project manager's technical skills as a project manager. It is important to understand why this situation has come about, what its effect is on the success of projects, and what can be done to remedy the situation.

We might ask that because project management is a relatively new profession, and that even today very few people come out of college or other training and education with the vocation of being a project manager, where have all of the project managers who are around today come from? The answer is: from the ranks!

The typical career path of a project manager begins in an area of expertise or knowledge, such as computer programming, business analysis, accounting, or operations. These people do what they do really well, and they understand the area in which they work very well. As a result, they are successful and advance in responsibility. Before you know it, they are leading other people in doing what they know how to do, because their knowledge and experience are so strong.

A few years ago, the term *project manager* started being used to define this function. Often, what they were doing was defined as simply "getting things done." In some ways, this is correct, but there is a hitch to this situation. In many, if not most, of these cases, when these project managers were transferred to another area completely, they would have a difficult time being successful, because what they became knowledgeable in and successful at was a product life cycle, not a project life cycle. A person who is very well versed in a product life cycle is not really a project manager, because this knowledge and expertise is in a specific subject matter, not in the project management process.

At times, it is possible to leverage subject matter expertise from one subject or knowledge area to another, but not all of the time. Project management expertise is always transferable from one knowledge area to another because it remains constant when the knowledge area changes.

The important difference to understand between product life cycle and project life cycle is this: The product life cycle determines the work that must be done in order to have a successful project in that knowledge area. It is the content of the project. The project life cycle ensures that

---

TIPS & TECHNIQUES

Project Life Cycle versus Product Life Cycle

Project Life Cycle

- Ensures that initiation, planning, execution, control, and closing are done properly.
- Requires project management skills.
- Determines the role of the project manager.

Product Life Cycle

- Determines what work must be done in order for the project to succeed.
- Requires technical or subject matter expertise.
- Determines the role of a technical team lead or subject matter expert.

the project is initiated and planned properly, executed and controlled properly, and closed properly.

When we understand the difference between the project life cycle and the product life cycle, we understand the difference between the project manager and the technical team lead or subject matter expert. This is crucial to project success. It is not a question of which is better or more competent. Actually, both roles are necessary for a successful project.

The technical team lead focuses on the area of knowledge in which the project takes place and works to ensure that everything is done according to the dictates of that area. The project manager works with the stakeholders and project team to ensure that the project is well planned and that all of the necessary activities are carried out in a timely fashion to complete the project successfully.

Project Initiation

As first mentioned in Chapter 2, project initiation is defined as "the process of formally authorizing a new project or that an existing project should continue into its next phase."[2] The purpose of project initiation can be broken down into eight separate themes, some of which are actual deliverables, whereas others are effects on the organization or the project. See Tips and Techniques, "Project Initiation."

When we analyze the definition of project initiation in the light of the purpose, let's first focus on the words *formally authorize*. This means that the organization gives formal approval for beginning the first phase of the project. We must note here that this formal authorization is narrow in scope; it only authorizes performing those activities that are proper to begin the project (i.e., setting direction, defining top-level objectives, defining requirements, securing approval and resources for the project, ensuring that the project is aligned with strategic objectives, assigning a project manager, and outlining the project manager's authority).

TIPS & TECHNIQUES

Project Initiation

- Formally authorizes the project to begin.

- Defines top-level objectives.

- Defines requirements.

- Secures approval and resources.

- Ensures alignment with the organization's strategic objectives.

- Identifies the project manager.

- Establishes the project manager's authority.

- Delivers the project charter.

The project charter contains all of this information and is also the main deliverable of project initiation. The activities required to complete a project charter are crucial to project success. When they are not accomplished, the project is most likely to suffer from lack of direction, a project that never ends, lack of buy-in from key stakeholders, or worse still, an irrelevant project whose deliverable gets put on the shelf when the project is finished. On time and on budget are good goals, but if the ensuing product or service is not utilized, it is still a waste of time, money, and other resources.

Project initiation does not require a large number of resources to carry out its activities. Actually, for most projects, only two or three resources are actively involved for the entire process. This should not minimize the importance of project initiation, which can be ignored only at the peril of project success. We have seen first hand in our training and teaching how the lack of effective project initiation is often the cause of project failure. Many project managers make comments such as, "That's why I'm having so much trouble on this project, I never did initiation properly" or "Now I see why I am having this problem."

The good news is that it is never too late to go back and do project initiation. When working on a troubled project, often the first thing an experienced project manager will do is either to review the project charter, or if one does not exist, develop it in order to see where the project should have been going.

Project Initiation Roles

According to *A Guide to the Project Management Body of Knowledge*,[3] the project sponsor is responsible for creating the project charter. Realistically, the project sponsor is often very busy and often not a project management professional. As a result, the sponsor may not understand the importance of the charter. Therefore, we usually recommend that the project charter be prepared by the project manager and approved by the project sponsor.

This can be a problem in an organization that delays naming the project manager until later in the cycle. Some organizations actually name one project manager for the feasibility study or initiation phase and then turn it over to another project manager once the project actually kicks off. When this is the case, the project manager must review the project charter rigorously, because it is the basis for all of the following project cycles.

If a project charter has not been completed when the project manager is assigned, even if the project is already well into the planning or even the execution phase, the project manager must still go back and create the project charter after the fact in order to ensure that the project is aligned to crucial business objectives.

Who should be the project sponsor? At the very least, the project sponsor should be an individual in the organization who is very familiar with the business objectives to which the project is related. Ideally, the project sponsor would be able to approve funds above and beyond the project manager's authority for the project.

There are those who say that the person who can approve or refuse funding is the real project sponsor, and there may be some truth to the statement. Without funding, projects do not move forward. At the very least, the project sponsor must be familiar with the manner in which projects are funded by the organization.

Another group of people are involved in the project charter: the project stakeholders. A stakeholder is anyone on whom the project will have an effect. The project sponsor, project manager, and approver of project funding are all stakeholders, but it goes much farther than that. All members of the project team are stakeholders, as is anyone who might ultimately be touched by the project, including end users.

If the project is external, then the client will have stakeholders as well. For an internal department, stakeholders will be found wherever the resulting deliverables have an impact. The real key at this stage of the project process is to understand which stakeholders can have influence on project approval and what that influence might be.

For example, there is a case where a project team in a functional organization did not consult with another department on a proposed project. The other department would not be affected by the project, but they *felt* as if they would be. The project sponsor did not consult this group of stakeholders, and they ultimately succeeded in getting the project cancelled. Although some stakeholders may not have to approve a project charter, it is important to seek support from any group that has the authority to keep a project from being approved.

The moral of the story here is to make sure that you find as many of the stakeholders as possible, in particular those who are not readily apparent, and then work with them as necessary to seek approval for the project.

The Project Charter

The Project Charter is the major deliverable in project initiation. The information gathered for it and the decisions that it documents will serve as the basis for the entire project. The project sponsor should normally create the project charter, but in our experience, we have found that the project manager will be the one to complete the work and then have the sponsor approve it. We recommend using the Strategic Project Charter Checklist and Template[4] (see Exhibit 3.2 as a way to ensure that no information is missing).

The first area that the project charter deals with is the roles involved in this project. We have already discussed the importance of the various roles, so all we need to note here is that the primary roles that should be included are the sponsor(s), the project manager, and the stakeholders. Each stakeholder notation should include comments about why they are a stakeholder, what their interest in the project is, and what influence they may have on the project. In some cases, the role of a steering committee that manages change control on a project may also be defined separate from stakeholders.

The next section of the charter deals with the project manager. This section should also outline the project manager's authority. Several types of authority are involved, including the authority to approve changes and budgets. In the case of the former, we are speaking about the limits of the project manager's authority to approve a change in schedule, budget, or resources. Usually, the project manager will have a limit to his or her authority to make changes in these project components without consulting the project sponsor or some other authority. Another type of authority needs to be explained, and we will digress a bit here in order to do so.

The triangle in Exhibit 3.3 represents a project, and each side of the triangle represents an aspect of the project. The three sides of the triangle

EXHIBIT 3.2

Strategic Project Charter Checklist

Checklist	Supporting Document
1. Who is issuing the strategic project charter?	
2. Is the issuer also a project sponsor?	
3. Who is (are) the client(s)? Who are the other stakeholders?	
4. Who is the project manager? What is the project manager's level of authority? Who does the project manager go to for decisions beyond his/her authority?	
5. Does the charter contain a statement of the mission and objectives of the sponsoring organization?	
6. Does the charter define the business needs that the project addresses?	
7. Does the project charter specify how the project is in alignment with the mission and objectives of the sponsoring organization?	
8. Does the charter contain high-level deliverables?	
9. Has a study been done to gauge the business impact of the project within the area where the project will take place? Within the organization at large?	
10. Has a study been done to gauge the business impact of the project outside of the organization (clients, partners, and suppliers)?	

EXHIBIT 3.2 CONTINUED

Checklist	Supporting Document
11. Has a financial analysis been done (ROI, sensitivity analysis)? Did they consider the full life cycle of the project product?	
12. Does the charter contain guidance as to how the project will be done?	
13. Is there a description of the conditions under which the project will take place?	
14. Does the charter state which management-level resources will be involved (at a minimum by skill set and area of expertise)?	
15. Does the charter contain an outline of the organization's responsibilities around resources and decisions?	
16. If the project is being performed under contract, has the contract been approved by the sponsoring organization? If it is internal, has it been approved by the organization?	
17. Does the charter contain clear statements of what constitutes success?	
18. Does the charter contain clear statements of how success will be measured?	

represent time, cost, and performance (which is also known as quality). This triangle is sometimes referred to as the Iron Triangle.

The Iron Triangle has certain characteristics; for instance, only one of the three sides can be rigid, whereas the other two must be flexible. For example, a project is going to create a new product, and the project plan states that it will take 175 working days for five people to complete the project if they all work full time.

Let's say that the Marketing department wants to launch the product in 120 days. The project manager realizes that this poses several problems that are found in the dynamic of the Iron Triangle. To shorten the time required to complete the project, either the resources must be increased (more personnel or more money) or the quality of the product must be decreased.

It may be more complex if the addition of resources cannot change the delivery date by 55 days. It could be that the areas of the manufacturing and safety testing processes cannot be shortened by the required time.

EXHIBIT 3.3

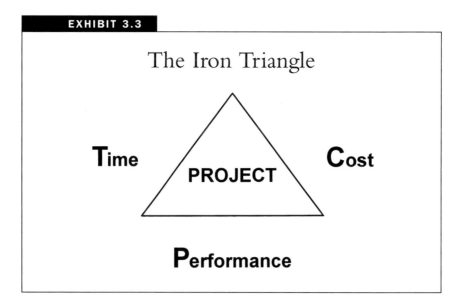

The Iron Triangle

Time

PROJECT

Cost

Performance

The project manager should have the authority in this type of situation to respond to the Marketing department that, within the limits of this project, we can make these changes to time, cost, and performance, but cannot go beyond that without significantly affecting the project. It may be, for example, that by increasing resources they can deliver the product in 140 days, but any less time than that will compromise quality unacceptably.

The project manager must, in this situation, have the authority to outline what the options are from which the Marketing department can choose. In many cases, this is not what happens; the project manager is overruled and given instructions to meet a certain date or certain level of spending that is not possible. The end result is a project that becomes a problem. Remember Frank Coleman's discussions on the Osterly project? It is important to understand that the project manager who does not have this authority is really a project coordinator or administrator. This is often the case in functional and weak matrix organizations.

The next section of the project charter deals with the business, its goals and objectives, and how the project aligns with them. The first requirement is a statement of business goals and objectives. Quite often, the formal published business goals and objectives of an organization are too long and complex for a project charter. What is needed here is a short, three- or four-sentence summary of how the company creates value (makes money!). An example of a business goals and objectives statement that is appropriate for a project charter may read like this:

> We create value by providing our customers with high-quality, moderately priced home appliances. Our service commitment to our customers is that in the unlikely event that they experience problems with their appliance, we will provide at-home service to the client the same day, if called by noon.

This is followed by a description of the business need or problem that the project is being created to solve. For the example of the appliance manufacturer, a business need could be something like this:

> It has become apparent that our service level for customer problem calls has not been meeting our commitment to our customers. In 42% of customer calls that arrive before noon, a service person does not arrive on the same day to handle the problem. As a result, we have had numerous customer complaints, and our ratings from the independent Customer Service Survey are below acceptable standards (90% rate us at 90% or better in the service category). Our present rating is only 63%.

Note that the description gets to the heart of the problem in a concrete way. More important, it provides quantifiable criteria that can serve as the basis for evaluating the success of any solution. Notice as well that the description of the problem does not yet involve a solution. That will come later in the charter. We can see clearly what the alignment will be between this project and the company's mission and objectives because we can see how the problem affects them.

As the problem has been stated, the project charter must contain the high-level deliverables that the project will produce. Defining these can be a bit difficult at times because we really don't know at this point exactly what the solution will look like. What we do know is what the results of the solution might look like. In other words, the high-level deliverables do not have to give exact details of what the project will produce—that happens in the planning phase.

What the high-level deliverables must show is what the desired results will look like. For the example we have been using, the high-level deliverables could look like this:

> The project will perform two studies that will produce a report detailing the reasons why the problems are occurring. The study

will cover all aspects of the Service Organization, including Inbound Call Center, Technology, Business Practices, Customer Service communications, and Personnel. The study will also determine the correlation between the present problem and the low service ratings. A second study will report on the actual appliance problems that are occurring, to see if the situation merits further investigation as to quality and manufacturing practices. Depending on the results of these studies, further action will be determined. Ultimately, we wish to return to a situation where 95% of all calls received before noon are serviced, and our Customer Service scores increase to 90% or greater.

This statement fits the criteria for high-level deliverables not only because it states clearly what the project is going to do, but also because it gives a clear indication of how success will be measured (using time delay for a service call made to a home and customer service ratings) and what results will be considered success (90% same-day service call rate and above 90% customer service rating).

At this point, we don't know what the actual deliverables will be; they could include new technology in the call center, new practices for handling calls, upgrading the skills of call center employees, or even hiring more service personnel. Even though we don't know what the outcomes will be, it is very clear what the desired *business result* is.

When we speak of the project as being in alignment with business mission and objectives, this example shows what we mean. The project is directly connected to the organization's mission, and its objectives will eventually contribute to increasing the organization's value, by improving customer service.

The next area addressed by the project charter is the impact of the project on the organization internally and externally. Information here includes the effect the project will have on everyone involved. If all of the stakeholders have not already been identified, this information will be difficult to complete. In some circumstances, it may not be possible to determine this information at this stage of the project. In particular, a multiphase project that will require much research and planning may not have all of the information necessary to complete the information at this stage.

When the project reaches the stage where the studies have been completed and decisions have been made regarding what changes will be made, information on what effect the project has internally and externally can then be made. This is a common occurrence in multiphase projects. The points at which decisions are made about how to proceed or whether to continue are called stage-gates, and the project charter is updated to facilitate decisions.

Another area the project charter addresses is the commitment of the organization to the project. This includes several facets, such as resources, both financial and people, and should at least give an indication of whether the project will need resources from outside the organization.

This commitment will depend on how this project compares to other projects in importance. Every organization has a limit to the amount of resources it possesses. Resources that are committed to this one project cannot be committed elsewhere. How that determination is made is a subject called portfolio management, which is covered in Chapter 8.

Suffice it to say here that the project charter must give an idea of what support can be expected, in order to facilitate planning. Later on, decisions may change about what is possible for the project to achieve, based on that commitment. The project charter can be amended at the time it passes through a phase-gate, depending on those decisions.

Summary

In this chapter, we've discussed the three types of organizational structure—functional, projectized, and matrix—what their characteristics are, and how to determine what type of organization structure your company has. We have also reviewed the crucial difference between project and product life cycle.

We have studied the project initiation process and the role of project sponsor, stakeholders, and project manager in this process, as well as reviewed how an organization's structure affects this process. We also looked at the importance of the project charter in the initiation process, identifying and describing the roles of various project stakeholders.

Finally, we did a detailed review of the project charter, explaining its importance to the project and describing its parts in great detail. Now, we are ready to start planning our project!

Endnotes

1. Janice Thomas, Connie L Delisle, Kam Jugdev, *Selling Project Management to Senior Executives* (Newton Square, PA: The Project Management Institute, 2002).

2. *A Guide to the Project Management Body of Knowledge* (Newton Square, PA: Project Management Institute, 2000).

3. Ibid.

4. The files are available on this book's companion Web site at *www.wiley.com/go/pm*.

CHAPTER 4

Project Planning

After reading this chapter you will be able to

- Understand what project planning is
- Appreciate why project planning is one of the two keys to project success
- Understand the proper sequence of project planning activities and how those activities are carried out
- Identify the roles involved in project planning
- Understand how different project planning tools are used to carry out project planning

Definition of Project Planning

Let us again turn to our experts for a definition of project planning. Before we look at them, however, we must note that *A Guide to the Project Management Body of Knowledge* (PMBOK)[1] does not contain a specific definition of project planning. The PMBOK lists a series of ten core processes and ten facilitating processes all involved in planning. Although the approach seems complex, it highlights the importance of project planning, which is often ignored in many organizations. For more information, please consult the PMBOK.[2]

Harold Kerzner[3] writes that project planning "includes three elements:

1. Definition of work products

2. Definition of quantity and quality of work

3. Definition of resources needed"

According to James P. Lewis,[4] project planning is "the answering of the following questions:

- What must be done?

- How should it be done?

- Who will do it?

- By when must it be done?

- How much will it cost?

- How good does it have to be?"

As we can see from the definitions, project planning is about getting ready to do a project. Although one definition uses formal language and the other informal, both definitions share several qualities. Both definitions are focused on what the project will deliver. This is a change in perspective from initiation. You will recall that during initiation, our focus was on linking business needs based on the organization's mission and goals to project outcomes. You will also recall that one of the results of initiation was high-level deliverables. The focus of project planning now shifts to expanding the details of the high-level deliverables and how they will be achieved. Both definitions also now focus on the Iron Triangle that was mentioned in the previous chapter: time, cost, and performance. Both definitions imply concerns about the quality of the deliverables, and finally both definitions bring resources into play—both the people who will do the work and other types of resources.

Project Planning Processes

The diagram in Exhibit 4.1 represents a high-level view of the project planning process. The tasks in the first row represent the primary project planning processes, and those in the second row represent secondary project planning processes. The last row contains the project plan, which is actually the major deliverable from the project planning process.

Primary Planning Processes

We refer to the first group of processes as primary processes because each of the processes must occur, and they generally must occur in the order in which they are listed, because each subsequent process depends on output from the prior process. There are always situations where these processes are repeated (more on this topic later in the chapter, when we discuss rolling wave), but before the project planning is complete, each process must be completed and its output used in the subsequent process. This will become clearer as we review the primary processes.

Secondary Planning Processes

Secondary processes support the primary processes, but they do not necessarily happen in a predetermined sequence. Some of these processes may or may not happen in a given project; for instance, a project that is

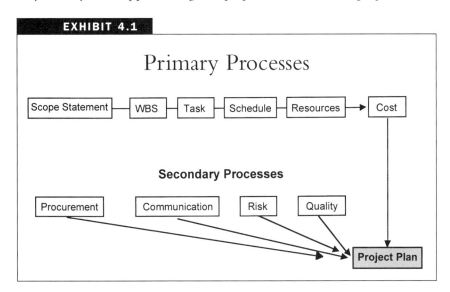

EXHIBIT 4.1

Primary Processes

Scope Statement — WBS — Task — Schedule — Resources → Cost

Secondary Processes

Procurement   Communication   Risk   Quality

Project Plan

not using any outside vendors or purchasing significant materials from outside the organization will probably not need a procurement process. However, quality and risk are almost always involved in every project.

Project Plan

The project plan is a compilation (often in electronic format) of the output of the planning process. On many occasions, the project plan is confused with the project schedule, which is actually a series of tasks in order of precedence. Many an inexperienced project manager will sit at an electronic tool and type a series of tasks into a Gantt chart and call it a project plan. Nothing could be further from the truth!

When properly prepared through the project planning process, a project plan is actually a detailed guide to executing and controlling a project. As you consider all of the work that goes into planning a project, you can begin to understand why the "Fire! Aim! Ready!" process of project execution leads to so many project disasters.

Project Scope Planning

Project scope planning is the process that delivers the scope statement, which is the crucial link between project initiation and project planning. In developing the scope statement, the project teams use the project charter, along with other information, to compose a high-level picture of what the project entails. Scope planning is the preliminary phase of project planning during which the project team gets ready to do the planning. In addition to the project charter, several other factors are considered during scope planning:

- *Assumptions.* Any condition that is known to be true that will affect a project. For example, when doing a software implementation project, assumptions must be made about the state of the hardware required for the implementation to be accomplished. The difference between having the hardware available and waiting and having no hardware at all will change project planning significantly. In a business process reengineering project, assumptions may be made about the state of current process documentation.

Completely undocumented processes will have a great effect on the level of resources needed to complete the project. A note of caution here: In common English, we often use the word *assume* to mean something we believe to be true but do not necessarily have confirmation of. In this case, *assumption* means something that we know and have verified to be true. We would not make an assumption about hardware without first verifying; nor would we assume that proper documentation existed without first studying the documentation to be sure. Assumptions often involve risk.

- *Constraints.* Any condition that may impede the progress of a project. For example, in a construction project, the availability of a subcontractor to pour concrete when needed may be a constraint. To return to the business process reengineering project, the availability of employees who are familiar with the processes undergoing reengineering may be a constraint. If they are busy doing their own work, they may not have enough availability to meet an aggressive project schedule. Constraints may also involve risk.

- *Project justification.* Why the project is needed. The justification will carry forward the link from the organization's strategic direction through the project charter and into planning.

- *Product/service description.* A more detailed description of the product or service to be delivered

- *Deliverables.* A more detailed listing of deliverables. Although it is not as detailed as the final description that will be developed during the rest of the planning process, at this point the deliverables must be detailed enough to define project completion. In other words, the deliverables must answer the question, how will we know when we are done? For example, in the software implementation project, the deliverables might look like this:

> At the end of the project, human resources generalists will be able to enter all personal and professional information concerning candidates who have been interviewed. In addition, the generalist will be able to initiate the system function that transforms a candidate into an employee in the system. After transformation, the new employee listing will contain all of the necessary information for that person to commence employment.

With this description, the organization has an idea of what it will take to complete the project; it may include business process work, software implementation and testing, and training. What they do know is how to judge the result.

- *Time, cost, and performance.* The scope statement should contain information, at least at a high level, about time, cost, and performance. Time and cost estimates may be made based on past experience and records (the reasons why project tracking and closing are so important), or if those records do not exist or this is a new area of work, outside expert information may be used.

The caveat here is that these are high-level, not detailed, estimates. They are used for general guidance around cost and time. They should be replaced by more accurate detailed estimates based on the detailed project planning process, which is discussed later in this chapter. Performance in this context refers to quality: how will we know what quality is when we see it? The answer is in the description of the deliverable service or product. When the product or service performs or is performed in the manner specified in the deliverable, we will have quality.

Finally, the scope statement also contains a listing of what the project *does not* include. This might seem a bit strange, but it is actually the first line of defense against scope creep (or scope gallop, as the case may be).

By explaining what the project is not, the most obvious areas that could create uncontrolled change can be, if not eliminated, at least identified as areas of concern.

When the scope statement is completed, it should normally be returned to the project sponsor for approval. It could be that other executive-level decision makers should also see and approve the scope statement. In some organizations, the scope statement is input to another process called project portfolio management. This process compares proposed projects with the organization's mission and objectives. Those projects that serve the organization's mission and objectives are then reviewed against available resources in order to see which projects can actually be accomplished. This topic is covered in more detail in Chapter 8.

Work Breakdown Structure

The work breakdown structure (WBS) is the spinal column of any project. The PMBOK defines the WBS as "a *deliverable*-oriented grouping

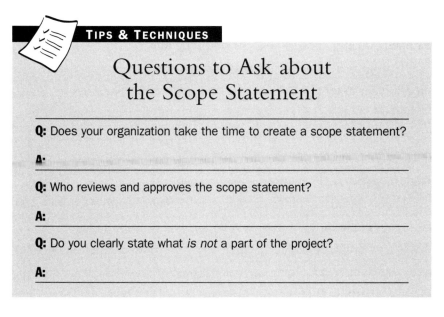

TIPS & TECHNIQUES

Questions to Ask about the Scope Statement

Q: Does your organization take the time to create a scope statement?

A:

Q: Who reviews and approves the scope statement?

A:

Q: Do you clearly state what *is not* a part of the project?

A:

of project elements that organizes and defines the total work scope of the project. Each descending level represents an increasingly detailed definition of the project work."[5]

The two keys here are that it is deliverable-oriented and increasingly detailed. The WBS is the primary planning tool that will transform the high-level deliverables into the individual work packages that will make up the project. The completed WBS will be used to do the following:

- Delineate work into specific activities.
- Assist in determining resources and their skill levels.
- Provide a foundation for estimating cost, resources, and time.
- Identify baselines for measuring performance.
- Provide a basis for project change control.

As you can see, the WBS is a crucial element in project planning. The end deliverable is a series of tasks that delineate *all* of the work to be done. We emphasize all because we mean that literally. Any work that is not described in the WBS is not considered to be part of the project. The work completed in the WBS serves as the basis for all the rest of the project planning process, including time and resource estimates, cost estimates, quality and risk analysis, and schedule.

If projects in your organization do not complete a WBS, then you should have an idea as to why time and cost estimates are not accurate. Whenever a project is late or over budget, the first question to ask is, "Do we have all of the planning details from the work breakdown structure?" If the WBS was not completed, then you have the answer. Without good, credible information, estimating accurately is not possible.

There are many different tools, both manual and electronic, and numerous methods for creating a WBS. We will describe a manual process that is very simple to use. It may be done with paper and pencil, on a flip chart or white board. Doing the manual process provides a basic concept of what a WBS is and how to create one, as well as a better understanding of why it is so important and what kinds of problems you may encounter when you don't do one. In its simplest form, a WBS resembles an organization chart, which most people are familiar with. It is simply a series of lines and boxes. Each level breaks the superior level down into more detail.

The top level of a WBS normally represents the entire project, and the second level is the high-level deliverables, as illustrated in Exhibit 4.2. If this were a software project, the high-level deliverables might include the major system components along with an implementation plan, the technical hardware and platform. In a new product development project, the high-level deliverables might include a concept, a prototype, and a production program. A training project might include needs analysis, training development, and delivery.

Alternately, if a project is large or expected to be of long duration, it may require a rolling wave strategy. A rolling wave strategy is used when there will be more than one trip through the project management process. Think back to the example of the home appliance manufacturer in Chapter 3. You may recall that the high-level deliverables included two studies: one to study the customer service problem and the other to determine if there were manufacturing problems as well.

The results of these studies would be used to determine the corrective steps that need to be taken. This is an example of the type of

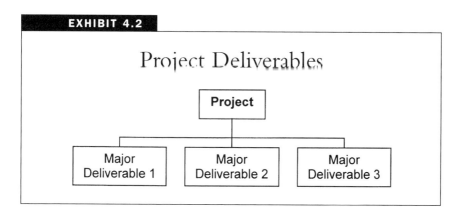

EXHIBIT 4.2

Project Deliverables

project that could use a rolling wave strategy. The second part of the project could be to take corrective action to improve customer service ratings. Until the studies are complete and have been properly analyzed, even the planning of the corrective action cannot begin. Therefore, a rolling wave strategy could be used.

The WBS for this project might start looking like Exhibit 4.3. As we can see in the illustration, all of the project cycle will take place in the study phase. Closing would still serve as a lessons learned activity, but it would also be the stage-gate to determine if the next phase should take place.

As you develop the WBS, a rule of thumb is that the general description of each element should be a noun until you reach the bottom level. You will know that you have reached the bottom level when you can describe an element with a verb.

In other words, the intermediate elements are always deliverables; the deliverables lower down make up the higher deliverables. The lowest level consists of the elements that describe the specific work that must take place to produce the deliverable. See Tips and Techniques, "Questions to Ask When Creating a WBS."

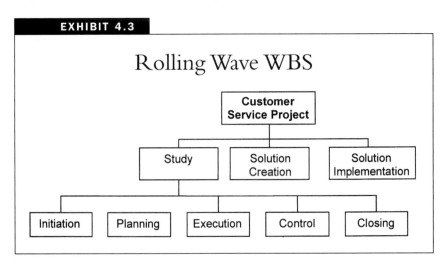

EXHIBIT 4.3

Rolling Wave WBS

TIPS & TECHNIQUES

Questions to Ask
When Creating a WBS

Q: Do all of the descending paths in the WBS contain about the same number of levels? If not, you may be missing work or have work in the wrong path.

A:

Q: Do you have any paths without branches? If so, there is either work missing or a deliverable has been broken down too small.

A:

Q: For each element: Can it be summarized by a noun?

A:

Q: For each element in the lowest level: Can it be summarized by a verb?

A:

Q: For each element: What is it? This provides the information needed to determine if the element is complete on delivery.

A:

Q: For each element: What does it do? This provides the information needed to determine quality on delivery.

A:

Q: When the WBS is complete, review each element and ask: Does this element equal the sum of the elements that make it up? Is anything missing from the elements below it? It is important to be sure that no work is missing.

A:

Once the WBS is completed, you will have all of the information needed to go on to the next phase, defining tasks.

Tasks

There are two terms that have various meanings in project management: *task* and *activity*. Depending on which source you consult, that meaning changes. For example, in the PMBOK an activity is the lowest level of the WBS, but it can be subdivided into tasks. From other experts, the opposite is true. For our purposes, we will say that there is no difference between a task and an activity, and our term of choice is task.

We define a task as a unit of work that takes one or two people no longer than two weeks to accomplish. Our definition is based on practical necessity. First of all, if work takes longer than two weeks to complete, you risk losing track of the work. The same holds true for two people. If more than two people are working on a task, then you need to break that task down further. Using two weeks as the time guideline also allows you to track your project more easily; you can track weekly to have a good feel for progress at any given time.

Defining tasks, like creating a WBS, is crucial to proper project planning. In particular, creating estimates of how long the project will take and what resources will be needed have their foundation in task definition. Task definition need not be complex. Following the Task Definition Form in Exhibit 4.4 will help make it easier. Let's take a closer look:

- *Task name.* Each task should have a name that describes its content. Often, tasks are labeled with a number of some sort. However, when the tasks multiply, remembering what a task is by a number is difficult. The name assigned to a task says what the task is about.

- *Task owner.* The task owner is the person who is responsible for seeing that the task is completed. The task owner is *not*

Task Definition Form

Task-Activity Description		
Task Name		
Task Owner		
WBS #		Resources Assigned
Start		
Duration		
Effort		
Dependencies		
Description		
Detailed Instructions (Note: The instructions should be detailed enough so that a team member with the proper skills and competencies can complete the task.)		

necessarily the person or persons who are accomplishing the task. For example, a technical team lead may be responsible for seeing that a series of programming tasks are complete, but the work is done by a programmer.

- *WBS #.* If your WBS has a numbering scheme, this number should correspond to the same element in the WBS. A note of caution: If you are not using software that automatically numbers the WBS for you, don't assign numbers until the WBS is complete. Invariably, the elements of a WBS are changed and moved. Renumbering every time you make a change is cumbersome and time consuming.

- *Start.* The date the task should be started on.

- *Duration and effort.* The duration is the time period (e.g., days, hours) the task should last. *Please note*: The duration should not be confused with effort. Effort is the amount of work the resources must do to complete the task. Duration is about elapsed time and does not necessarily correspond to effort.

For example, a resource may work on a task 4 hours per day. There may be a constraint that says that the person cannot work on the task on Tuesdays. That means the resource is working on the task 16 hours per week. If the task takes 32 hours of effort, the duration will be two weeks. Conversely, if two people work 4 hours each day on the same task that requires 32 hours, they will complete the task in 4 days.

If you have a great deal of experience in the type of project you are planning, it is much easier to estimate the effort required for each task. The records and lessons learned from previous projects and the expertise of project team members are important inputs into the estimating process.

If you do not have a great deal of expertise in the area the project is addressing or lack records of previous projects, you can consult with

TIPS & TECHNIQUES

Duration versus Effort

Duration

The time period that a task should last. It may be calculated in hours or days. Duration represents elapsed time. It may be that a 15-hour task will occur over a period of two weeks; that is duration.

Effort

The amount of work the resources must do to complete the task. For example, a task may take 15 hours to complete; that is effort.

outside sources that do. If none of those alternatives are available to you, then the team must make their best possible estimate under the circumstances. Later on, when the project team addresses risks, the manner in which estimates were done should be taken into consideration.

As the project progresses, the schedule can be adjusted according to the results you are achieving. It is better to recognize the risks of poor information for estimating at this point, and address it in the project risk plan, than to ignore the issue completely.

- *Dependencies.* These are any tasks that must be completed in order for this task to be completed. For example, if you are developing a new product, the team building a prototype cannot begin until the design has been completed.

- *Description.* The description is a short paragraph that briefly summarizes the answers to the questions "What is it?" and "What does it do?" from the WBS.

- *Detailed instructions.* The detailed instructions give directions to the person or persons completing the task. These instructions assume that the resources are competent to perform the task, and should only contain enough detail so that the competent person can complete the task. The detailed instructions often contain references to other documents and materials needed to complete the task.

- *Resources assigned.* During the early stages of project planning, you may not know yet which resources will be working on the task. If not, it is important to either indicate the skill sets needed to complete the task or provide a position description (e.g., programmer or sheet metal worker).

It is not unusual for a project team to lack some information needed to fill in sections of the task description at this point, in particular about resources, effort, and duration. Remember that project planning is a repetitive process, and it is possible that you may review task descriptions several times before they are complete. It may be that you will need to work on scheduling and resources and then return to task descriptions later on.

Now that the tasks are defined, at least in the first draft, we can move on to resources.

Resources

Now that the tasks have been defined and the preliminary estimates on resources—or at least the skill sets needed—have been compiled, the next step is to determine the actual resources needed to complete the project. There are a series of questions to be answered concerning internal resources, their availability, and their level of skills that will guide the planning process.

The answers to these questions will affect the project schedule. In many organizations, the availability of resources is the primary issue surrounding projects. Often, projects are mandated for which there simply are not enough resources available, or employees who must also do their regular jobs are assigned to projects. We will address these issues in Chapter 8 when we discuss portfolio management.

Scheduling

Turning a series of tasks, duration and resource estimates, and other information into a realistic project schedule can be a daunting task. In some organizations, project scheduling is a full-time job all by itself. We will cover the main points of the process of creating a schedule; however, for those who wish to delve deeper into this topic, see the section on critical path calculation later in this chapter. There are many different software tools available now to facilitate project scheduling. Rarely is this done manually any more. However, understanding the underlying principles will help you understand how a project schedule works.

Questions to Ask When Assigning Resources to a Project

Ask yourself these questions:

Q: Are there internal resources with the proper skill sets?

A:

Q: Are these resources available to the project?

A:

Q: If not, can other employees be trained in the proper skill?

A:

Q: If external resources are needed, can the project budget support their use?

A:

Q: Will the external resources be hired as full-time employees or will they be temporary? Will a vendor be used?

A:

Q: Will subject matter or technical experts from other areas of the organization be needed? If so, what availability will be needed?

A:

Often, a project team is placed in a challenging situation: a project is announced, including the deliverables and the end date, and handed over to the project team. At the same time, the project delivery date is also announced. Here's the catch: If the team has not yet done the detailed planning, including scheduling, that project date is a wish! The problem is that project teams are often held accountable for that wish.

Proper project scheduling can greatly improve the likelihood of a project finishing on time.

The first step in scheduling is creating a network diagram of the tasks to be accomplished. Again, this is normally done with software, but it can be done manually for smaller projects. This is nothing more than arranging the tasks in the order in which they will be done. The tasks are placed in order of precedence, meaning that a task that depends on another task should be placed after the task it depends on (see Exhibit 4.5).

The arrows between the tasks show the order in which the tasks will be performed and which task depends on which. At times, more than one task may depend on a previous task, which is indicated by diverging arrows (see Exhibit 4.6).

These two tasks could very well reconverge on another task, or they could continue as parallel paths in the project schedule. Having tasks running in parallel paths is one way to get things done more efficiently during a project, as long as there are sufficient resources to do all of the tasks. In larger projects, it is not unusual to have many paths diverging and reconnecting throughout the project (see Exhibit 4.7). The other advantage of a network diagram is that you can easily follow a path through the project and understand how the various tasks depend on one another. Recall the Iron Triangle: parallel tasks are one way to shorten the time side of the Iron Triangle.

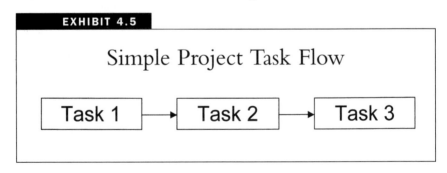

EXHIBIT 4.5

Simple Project Task Flow

Task 1 ⟶ Task 2 ⟶ Task 3

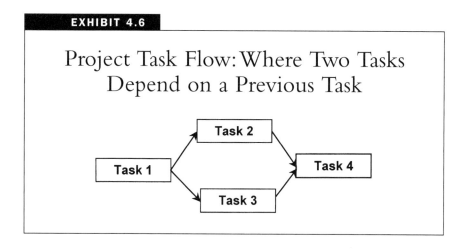

EXHIBIT 4.6

Project Task Flow: Where Two Tasks Depend on a Previous Task

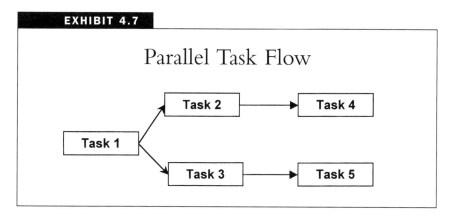

EXHIBIT 4.7

Parallel Task Flow

Once the network diagram is complete, the duration and effort numbers are applied to the diagram in order to calculate the end date of the project. Two calculations are done; the first measures time from the beginning of the project to the end. This establishes the finish date. Then the diagram is recalculated from the finish date to the beginning of the project. This enables you to see how much float there is in the project. Float is the amount of leeway that any task might have between when it may be finished and when it must be finished in order not to delay a task that follows it.

Calculating Critical Path

Creating a project schedule and calculating the critical path are the two crucial steps to determine the length of a project. It is very likely that you will never calculate a critical path manually (after you are done reading this section!), but knowledge of how it is calculated will help you make sense of a project schedule in the future. No matter how large or complex a project is, the calculation is always the same, but most project teams will likely do such calculations with a software tool. We will do a quick overview and then show the detailed calculations.

There are three steps to calculating the critical path:

1. *Calculating the forward pass.* This calculation determines two dates for each task: the early start date and the early finish date. The early start date is the earliest date that a task could start, based on when the previous task finishes. The early finish date is the earliest date that a task can finish, given the earliest start date and the duration of the task. The forward pass starts with the first task in the project's network diagram and proceeds in sequence to the last task. The early finish date of the last task is also the earliest possible end date for the whole project.

2. *Calculating the backward pass.* This calculation determines the late start date and late finish date for each task. The late start date is the latest date that a task can start without delaying the start of the next task in sequence. The late finish date is the latest that task can finish also without delaying the next task in sequence. The backward pass begins with the last task in the project and proceeds backward through the project in sequence. The late start date of the first task in the project is the latest date that the project can start without delaying the end date of the project.

3. *Calculating the critical path.* We calculate the critical path by first determining the float in each task. This is done by subtracting

either the early start date from the late start date or the early finish date from the late finish date in each task. The float in each task indicates the amount of time a task may be delayed without affecting the end date of the project. As an example: If a task has four days float, then it can be delayed by up to four days without affecting the end date of the project. If a task has zero days float, then any delay in the task will delay the end date of the project. The critical path is simply the series of tasks throughout a project that have zero float (see Exhibit 4.8).

Forward-Pass Calculations

To calculate the forward pass, we start at the left-most task and perform the following:

Early Start + Duration − 1 = Early Finish

If the first activity starts on Day 1 and lasts for 2 days, then early start is 1 and the early finish is 2. This means that the earliest day the task could start on is Day 1 (of course!), and the earliest day that it could finish is Day 2.

Now that we have finished with the first task, we must calculate the early start date of the next task. To do that, we calculate:

Early Finish + 1 = Early Start

Following the previous example, if the early finish of the first task were 2, then the earliest day that the next task could begin would be Day 3. We are ignoring weekends and holidays that could change the schedule. Most software programs would track these days automatically.

What would we do then, when a single task is followed by multiple tasks? It's not hard. Each of the subsequent tasks follows the same formula (see Exhibit 4.9):

Early Finish + 1 = Early Start

EXHIBIT 4.8

Key Definitions for Calculating Critical Path

Early Start Date (ES)	Earliest possible point in time an activity can start, based on the network logic and any schedule constraints.
Duration	Number of work periods, excluding holidays or other nonworking periods, required to complete the activity; expressed as workdays or workweeks.
Early Finish Date (EF)	Earliest possible time the activity can finish.
Forward Pass	Starting at the beginning (left) of the network, develop early start and early finish dates for each task, progressing to the end (right-most box) of the network.
Late Start Date (LS)	Latest point in time that an activity may begin without delaying that activity's successor. If the activity is on the critical path, the project end date will be affected.
Float or Slack	Latest point in time a task may be delayed from its earliest start date without delaying the project finish date.
Late Finish (LF)	Latest point in time a task may be completed without delaying that activity's successor. If the activity is on the critical path, the project end date will be affected.
Backward Pass	Calculate late start and late finish dates by starting at project completion, using finish times and working backward.

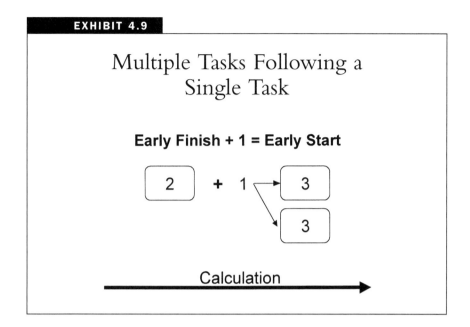

EXHIBIT 4.9

Multiple Tasks Following a Single Task

Early Finish + 1 = Early Start

Calculation

But what do we do when two activities precede one? In that case, the early start of the successor activity is based on the latest of the early finish dates of the predecessor. If you look at Exhibit 4.10, you can see that Task B finishes *later than* Task C; therefore, the early start of Task D is calculated using Task B. In this example, Task D would start on Day 18.

You simply continue calculating the forward pass until you reach the end of the project.

Backward-Pass Calculations

Let's begin calculating the backward pass with the last task in the project. Don't forget that we are calculating in the opposite direction. We start with the finish date of the project, according to the forward pass, and calculate (see Exhibit 4.11):

Late Start = Late Finish – Duration + 1

EXHIBIT 4.10

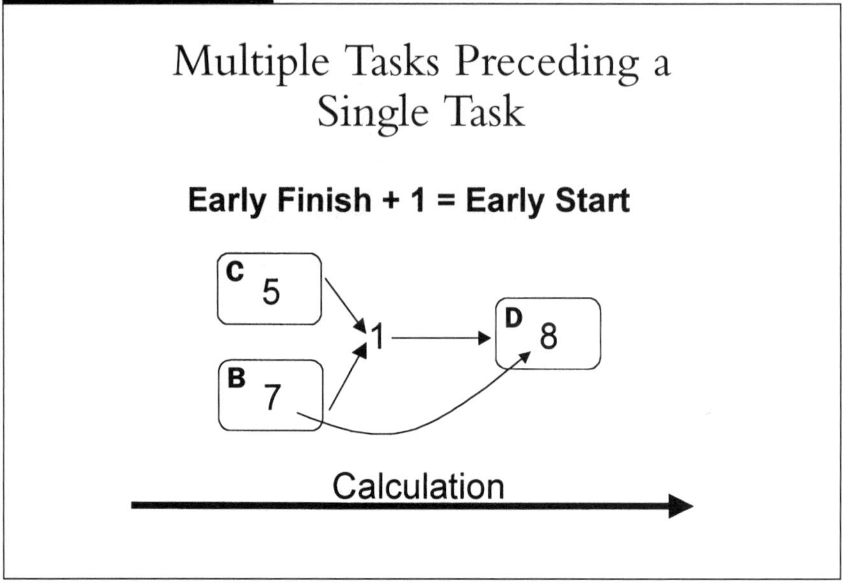

Multiple Tasks Preceding a Single Task

Early Finish + 1 = Early Start

Calculation →

EXHIBIT 4.11

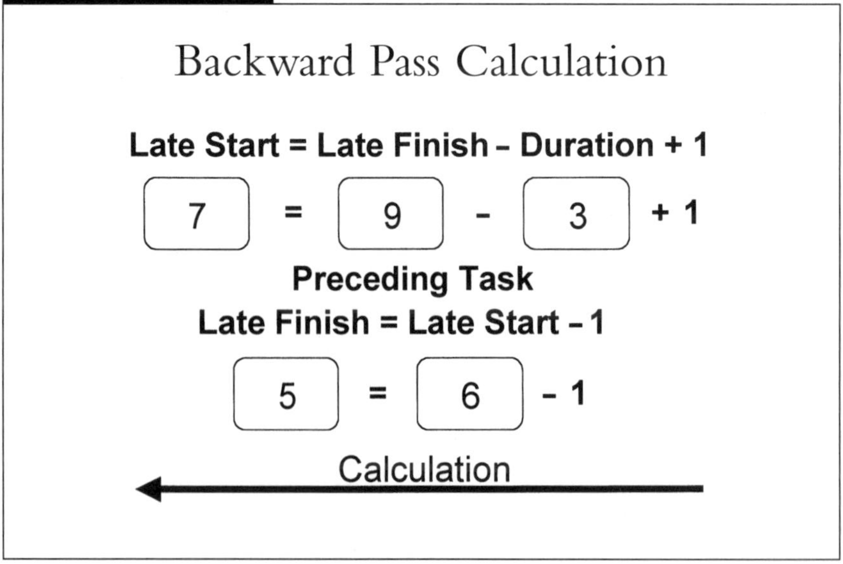

Backward Pass Calculation

Late Start = Late Finish – Duration + 1

$$7 = 9 - 3 + 1$$

Preceding Task

Late Finish = Late Start – 1

$$5 = 6 - 1$$

← Calculation

To calculate the late finish of the preceding task, we simply take the late start of the task in question and calculate:

Late Start − 1 = Late Finish

As with the forward pass, when calculating backward pass, we must deal with tasks that converge and diverge. For converging tasks, the late finish of the preceding tasks are both calculated based on the late start of the following task (see Exhibit 4.12).

For diverging tasks, the late finish of the earlier task is based on the earliest of the late start dates of the successor (see Exhibit 4.13).

The backward pass continues until it is calculated all the way to the beginning of the project.

Critical Path Calculations

Now that we have calculated both the forward and backward passes, we must determine the float in the project. Float determines the amount

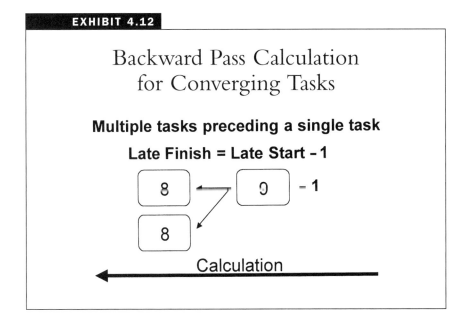

EXHIBIT 4.12

Backward Pass Calculation
for Converging Tasks

Multiple tasks preceding a single task

Late Finish = Late Start - 1

8 ← 9 − 1

8

Calculation

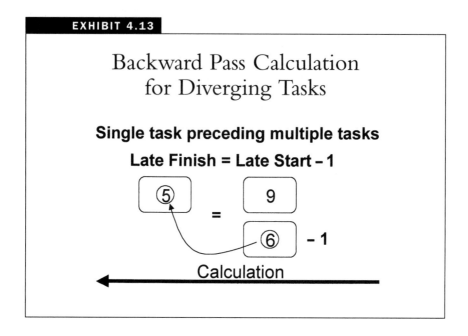

EXHIBIT 4.13

Backward Pass Calculation for Diverging Tasks

Single task preceding multiple tasks
Late Finish = Late Start – 1

of flexibility (time) each activity can move without affecting the network schedule end date. We calculate float as either:

Float = Late Finish – Early Finish

or

= Late Start – Early Start

If the resulting number is greater than zero, this means movement is available. If, for example, a task has a positive float of 4, the task can be delayed up to three days without affecting the next task in line (see Exhibit 4.14).

If the number is equal to zero, then any delay in this task means that the end date of the project will be affected (see Exhibit 4.15).

The critical path consists of the series of tasks with zero float throughout the project. Any delay in any of these tasks will delay the end date of the project. Total float is the amount of time that tasks can be delayed before they delay the end date of the project. In Exhibit 4.16, the critical

Calculating the Float

LS – ES = Float
LF – EF = Float

ES · · · · · · · · · · · · EF
5 · · · · · · · · · · · · 8

9 - 5 = 4
12 - 8 = 4

9 · · · · · · · · · · · · 12

LS · · · · · · · · · · · · LF

Float = 4

Sample Calculation Where Float Equals Zero

LS – ES = Float
LF – EF = Float

ES · · · · · · · · · · · · EF
6 · · · · · · · · · · · · 10

6 - 6 =
10 - 10 =

6 · · · · · · · · · · · · 10

LS · · · · · · · · · · · · LF

Float = 0

EXHIBIT 4.16

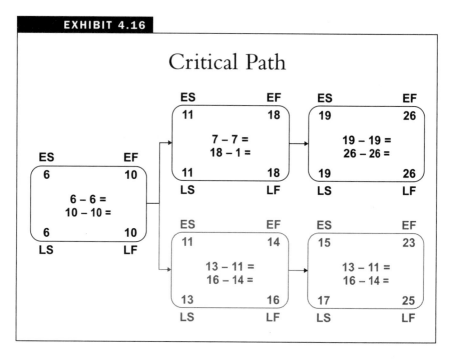

Critical Path

path is indicated in the bold outline. Each task in the critical path has a float of zero.

The critical path is the path of tasks that has no float, so that a delay in any one of these tasks would delay the project. The finish date of the project is at the end of the critical path. Any delay in a task on this path will delay the end of the project, so that you must pay close attention to the tasks on the critical path.

We cannot stress enough that this calculation is the *only* way to get a realistic and accurate idea of what a project's duration will be. As the calculations are done, consideration must be made for resource availability; a task that should start on a particular date but cannot because a resource is not available will be constrained to start only when the resource is available. When the calculations are complete, the finish date of the project will be known. The finish date will be much more reliable than a date that is mandated out of necessity.

IN THE REAL WORLD

Something's Got To Give
(Critical Path War Story)

One of the most common and critical mistakes you can make in planning a project is to mandate a project end date before the entire scope and work effort of the project is really known. This is a typical practice within organizations that are trying to do too much too quickly and are striving for significant revenue gains without considering the hidden expenses that improper project planning and continual scope changes can generate.

For example, in one organization, the vice president of a business mandated that a new revenue opportunity (strategic) needed to be rolled out within a 90-day time frame (tactical and operational). The project manager who had been assigned to this project held a meeting with all of the stakeholders to discuss the project scope and then followed up with a working session in which each stakeholder outlined major tasks, estimated the duration and effort involved for subprojects, and identified dependencies across subprojects.

Once this effort was complete, it was clear that the duration and dependencies of the tasks would drive the end date of the project well beyond the 90 days initially mandated by the vice president. In addition, the critical path of the project indicated there was little float on the schedule at all, representing significant risk to completion of the project on time, on budget, and to the performance desired.

Once this savvy and experienced project manager conveyed the potential risks of adhering to such an unrealistic time frame (i.e., increased costs and reduced quality), the sponsor agreed that the timeline could be extended to really reflect what work would need to be done.

If you remember the three sides of the Iron Triangle—time, cost, and performance—you will also remember we mentioned that project managers must be able to control at least one of these elements or they really aren't managing a project, they are simply coordinating it and subject to the effects of scope gallop.

What actually controls the finish is the Iron Triangle of time, cost, and performance (quality). The finish date of the project represents the deliverables as they are defined in the project charter. In other words, this is the date that the deliverables will be finished at this cost with this level of quality.

Although techniques are available to tweak the project schedule, major changes in the finish date will have to be realized through changes in at least one, if not all, sides of the Iron Triangle. You may move the finish date by increasing cost (i.e., using more resources).

This will usually only work to a point, because some tasks may not respond to increased resources. In a construction project, if concrete must be cured for two weeks, adding more resources to the project will not decrease the amount of time for curing.

You may also move the date by lowering quality; it may be possible that you are delivering more quality than is necessary. For example, in software development projects, designers often include a few bells and whistles that they feel the customer may like, even if they are not required. However, this may also increase cost and should be eliminated from the project. In the long run, the best way to overcome late projects is to plan and schedule properly, and not to commit to a finish date before the planning is done!

Cost Estimation

Estimating project costs can seem to be very difficult. The difficulty may come from two sources: size and information. Very large projects will have complex cost estimates. There are many software tools out there to help with cost estimating on large projects. However, always remember that cost estimating is done at the task level of detail. The cost of a task is equal to the effort multiplied by the rate of the assigned resources. The other source of difficulty can be a lack of information about the project.

Let's pause at this point, and look back at what information project planning has given us:

- Detailed deliverables with notations about what they are and what they do
- A set of tasks that describe the work necessary to complete the deliverables
- A list of resource needs to complete the tasks, including personnel and other resources (e.g., equipment, software, space, and other)
- Estimates of the effort needed from the resources to complete the tasks
- A list of constraints about resources needed, including availability, and the need for training
- A schedule of when each task will start and be completed, creating the finish date

All of this information becomes input into the cost estimating process.

Next, let's determine the internal costs for the project; we will address external costs later. To begin with, we look at the cost of project personnel. If you have determined that the organization has all of the proper resources internally, and that all of them have the proper skill sets, then you do not need to account for training. To determine the cost of any person, you simply multiply the number of hours that the person will work on the project by the hourly rate that the person costs the organization.

Sounds simple, right? Other considerations must be taken into account here. First of all, if the person is not an hourly employee (and most are not these days), you must at least have an estimate of what that person costs on an hourly basis (including benefits, taxes, and other). Many organizations feel that this is confidential information, so they create estimates for a band or type of employee. These estimates will suffice.

You should also consider the employee's skill sets. A newer employee with less experience may take longer to do a particular task than a more experienced person. In this case, you may want to adjust the effort required for the task before estimating the cost. It would not be difficult to create a table or spreadsheet in order to calculate this information.

If you must hire from the outside, other questions come into play. Will you hire full-time employees or temporary contractors? Will you use an outside vendor? If you hire employees, will the cost of hiring be borne by the project? Will the cost of training be borne by the project? If present employees must be trained, will that cost be borne by the project? Once these questions have been answered, you may then calculate the additional costs and include them in the estimate.

In closing this section, it is important to remember that the key to cost estimating and management is adequate information. Without understanding in detail the project deliverables and the work tasks necessary to produce them, no cost estimate will stand up for very long. Without accurate information about the project schedule, tracking cost becomes very difficult as well.

Quality Planning

Over the last few years, quality has become big business. Total quality management (TQM), continuous improvement, Six Sigma, International Standards Organization (ISO), and many others have become a part of corporate culture. Many professional organizations address the quality issue. We cannot, nor would we want to try to, cover all of those issues in this section. What we would like to do is explain the concept of quality in the context of project management, which is not all that complex in theory. We would also like to give you some guidelines for implementing quality in your projects.

To begin with, let's define some concepts regarding quality:

- *Quality management.*[6] The processes undertaken to ensure that a project will satisfy the needs for which it was undertaken

- *Quality planning.* Identifying which quality standards are relevant to the project and determining how to satisfy them

- *Quality assurance.* Evaluating overall project performance regularly to provide confidence that the project will satisfy the relevant quality standards

- *Quality control.* Monitoring specific project results to determine if they comply with relevant quality standards and identifying ways to eliminate causes of unsatisfactory performance.

There is often confusion among the different elements of quality, particularly between quality control and quality assurance. As we can see from the previous definition, quality management includes quality planning, quality assurance, and quality control. Generally speaking, the minimalist rule that we have applied to other concepts of project management should apply here as well. Quality management should consist of those procedures that will ensure that the project fulfills the needs it was intended to—no more and no less.

Quality management is not an end in itself, but a means to an end. Depending on the industry and project, many different quality standards may apply. The pharmaceutical industry is a case in point; Food and Drug Administration (FDA) regulations are, of necessity, complex and difficult to follow. They ensure the safety of the many drugs we use. Our point here is that these quality standards should be applied in the context of project management. The special regulations or standards of any industry are addressed as part of quality management on any project where required. Consider that the cost of prevention is usually less than the cost of correction.

The basis of quality planning is the two simple questions that were asked as part of creating the WBS. For each element of the WBS, we asked:

1. What is it?

2. What does it do?

Although this may seem almost too simple, it is the right place to start.

The first criterion of quality is whether the deliverable is what it is supposed to be. During quality planning, you must take up the answer to this question and decide how you would know if the end deliverable was what it is supposed to be. On a technical project, this might involve a comparison with the detailed specification of a product or software. On a nontechnical project (e.g., a project to reengineer a business process), this would be a comparison with the proposed workflow of the new process.

The second part of the quality planning process is determining how you will know that the deliverable is doing what it is supposed to do. This can be as simple as a run-through of a new business process to the detailed and lengthy testing done on new pharmaceutical products. Use the questions in Tips and Techniques, "Quality Management Questions to Ask," to help you with this work.

The final phase of project planning is to develop the procedures that will be used to monitor quality during the project. This includes both the actual tests for quality that will be conducted (quality control) and the manner in which the project will be monitored to ensure quality (quality assurance).

Risk

Planning for and dealing with risk is never easy. How do you plan for what you don't know? This might sound funny, but it is true that if you know that something in particular will go wrong with a project, it is not a risk. Risk refers to those things that can go wrong with a project that are unknown.

TIPS & TECHNIQUES

Quality Management
Questions to Ask

Can it be produced?

A:

Is it what the client wants?

A:

Will they pay its cost?

A:

Will it be useful?

A:

Will it be reliable?

A:

Will it be maintainable?

A:

Will it be affordable?

A:

Who is responsible for quality activities?

A:

What processes will be used?

A:

How will documentation be kept?

A:

What are the standards for measurement?

A:

How and when will corrective action be taken?

A:

There are two types of unknowns: the known unknown and the unknown unknown. We are not just playing with words here. We mentioned previously that if you know that something will go wrong with a project, it is not a risk because you can plan ahead of time how to deal with it. However, there are things that could possibly go wrong with your project, and you know what they are but not whether they will happen or not. These are known unknowns. The second category of unknowns is things that could go wrong but you don't know what they are, so you cannot know if they will happen. The latter category is usually uncontrollable events such as weather, which are normally mitigated with insurance.

Risk planning deals with the known unknowns. It is the process of defining potential risks and the ways in which you will both mitigate their occurrence and respond if they actually do occur. The results of this work are called a risk management plan: the comprehensive manner in which you will identify and plan for how to deal with risk. This should not be confused with a risk response plan, which addresses the responses that will be made to individual risks.

In review, risk management includes the following steps:

1. *Risk identification.* Systematically identifying all possible risks

2. *Risk qualification.* Judging the probability that a risk will occur, and if it does, how serious a threat it poses to the project

3. *Risk mitigation planning.* What you will do to prevent identified risks from occurring

4. *Risk response planning.* What you will do if a risk actually occurs

5. *Risk management plan development:*
   - Documenting roles and responsibilities
   - Budgeting (contingency dollars and insurable risk)

- Threshold criteria
- Reporting and tracking

An important aspect of risk planning is *who* will be involved. Normally, the entire project team should be involved in risk planning. The input of all team members will be important for successful risk planning. Other stakeholders may also want to have input into risk planning. If available, the project sponsor can often provide valuable input into risk planning from the organization's perspective. In client projects, representatives from the client team and other stakeholders should also be included.

Following our minimalist rule, risk planning does not need to be very involved. It can be as simple as the entire project team brainstorming possible risks together and then analyzing their likelihood and severity on a simple scale. Using the WBS, project schedule, and task descriptions, team members could individually identify risks and classify them on a 1 to 5 scale, based on how likely they are to occur and how severe the impact would be if they did occur.

Once this work has been completed, team members would each take several of the identified risks and answer two questions about them: (1) what will we do to prevent this risk from happening (mitigation) and (2) what will we do if the risk does occur (response).

The answers to these questions would be reviewed by the team and compiled into the risk response plan. The project manager would then be responsible for seeing that the risk management plan was followed.

Project Communication Planning

Project communication management is defined as "the process required to ensure timely and appropriate generation, collection, dissemination, storage, and ultimate disposition of project information. It provides the critical links among people, ideas, and information that are necessary for success."[7] In this section, we focus on the planning aspect of communication management.

It is important to understand that project communications involves a great deal more than communications between project team members. Project communications involves all stakeholders in the project. You will recall that in Chapter 2, we defined a stakeholder as any person who will either be affected by the project or who can have an effect on the project. In a sense, project communications is almost like a project within a project. It must be initiated, planned, executed, controlled, and closed.

The key to project communications planning is identifying all stakeholders and understanding what information they need to receive, as well as what information you may need from them. Once you understand the communication needs, you can decide how you will approach each stakeholder (what channel). For example, will you use printed media or electronic communication? If you use electronic, will it be e-mail or another type of communication?

One example to consider here is the communication of internal information and documentation among project team members. E-mail may seem to be the easiest way to do this, but consider how you will control the versions of the documentation. E-mail circulation can quickly spread different versions of documents, leading to serious problems. Another problem with e-mail is capturing the sequence of messages in order to understand what is really being communicated.

For internal communications within a project, sometimes a controlled database is a better communications tool. Not only will it help control the versions of project documents, but some databases will also allow for threaded messages so that project team members can see the progression of messages more easily.

You must also consider communications outside of the project team. Those who will ultimately be affected by the project will need information about what is happening and how the project will affect them. The project sponsor and any other management or executive person who can have an effect on the project will need information. Each of these groups will require a different type of information.

The project sponsor may need detailed project status information, whereas executives will need a less detailed account of project progress. Employees or clients who will be affected by the project will need details about when and how the project will affect them. This may be as simple as a notice or as complicated as a detailed instruction manual or a training course of some sort. Exhibit 4.17 contains a checklist of all the activities required in communications planning. In the Real World, "Mitigating Risk with Communications" provides an excellent example of how project communications overcame the most serious potential risk to a project by using the higher-level project stakeholders as a crucial communications link.

Project Procurement Planning

The PMBOK[8] defines project procurement management as "a subset of Project Management that includes the processes required to acquire goods and services to attain project scope from outside the performing organization." Organizations must often acquire resources from the outside, both materials and people. Once you have decided to acquire resources from the outside, it is important to consider the organization's methods for acquiring outside resources in the project planning process. If your organization has a procurement process, what effect will that process have on your project?

Timing is one consideration. If it takes two months to bring a new vendor on, and you must have the work completed in six weeks, you will have a problem. However, you may have a list of preferred vendors, but there may not be a vendor on the list that can fulfill your need. In that case, it may take time to bring a new vendor onto the preferred list, not to mention finding a vendor that suits your needs.

You must also consider cost. Outside resources are less expensive in some cases than inside resources. For example, if a company does not have a subject matter expert to join the project team of a three-month project, it may be less expensive to bring in a contractor for the three months than to hire a new person full-time, in particular if there is no need for the expert after the project. In the case of some materials, it

Communications Planning Summary

Emergency Communications Process	A description of the process and modes to be used for emergency communications.
Tools	A list of the communication tools used to implement the communications plan: e-mail, brochure, newsletter, bulletin boards, demonstrations, presentations, meetings, and status reports.
Resources	Resources that are required to implement the communications plan. This includes personnel and financial resources.
Issues	A list of the issues based on risk analysis, as well as the risk response plan.
Key Success Indicators	List the success indicators for the communications strategy, including actual performance against planned schedule and budget, including ways that the effectiveness of the strategy will be measured.
Evaluation	Regular evaluation of the communications strategy will be done according to the success indicators. Evaluations will be done at key intervals (milestones and deliverables) throughout the project, including project closeout.

Mitigating Risk with Communications

TAP Pharmaceuticals Products Inc. (TAP) is a major provider of pharmaceutical products. Recent success has been at the root of rapid growth in size, adding thousands of employees. In order to better serve the organization's human resources needs, TAP had implemented an Employee Resource Planning (ERP) solution. However, when the system was not living up to expectations, the new manager of Human Resources Information Systems, Marianne Mertes, decided to take a closer look.

TAP Pharmaceuticals, like any organization, had established processes and methods for human resources. When a new information technology system is implemented, the point at which the established processes meet the new system is usually where most problems will arise, because the established process often doesn't match the system requirements.

As an example, many ERP systems now allow the recruiting function of Human Resources to enter candidate information, thereby allowing a smoother transition when a new employee is hired. Rather than keeping a lot of paper and making multiple entries, when an employee is hired, the system moves the new employee from candidate status to employee status. The problem might arise during the interview process, if all of the information needed for an employee is not collected on the candidate's application, thereby delaying candidate entry into the system. Multiply this one simple problem by the number of processes that exist and the information they capture, and you have the potential for complex problems.

It was clear that without changes to business processes, TAP's ERP system could not function as effectively as it should. Ms. Mertes put together a project team to deal with the changes. This was a daunting task, because change is never easy, and a great deal of change to well-established processes can cause chaos.

IN THE REAL WORLD CONTINUED

During the planning phase of the project, the project team analyzed the risks associated with process change and realized that the biggest risk factor was the availability of numerous employees from outside of Human Resources to work as subject matter experts (SMEs). The SMEs' input would be crucial to accurately mapping existing processes and creating new processes. The team decided to use communications to mitigate the risk.

Rather than contact either employees or their managers directly, the team decided to create a communications campaign that would address the company at two levels. First, all company employees would be informed of what would be happening and what the benefit to them would be.

Second, the Vice President of Human Resources, Denise Kitchen, would communicate with the vice presidents of all other divisions within TAP. Ms. Kitchen not only informed them of the benefits of the project, but she also collaborated with the other vice presidents to commit resources to the project. The vice president informed the employees chosen for the SME role in the project via the employee's own manager.

The vice presidents were also asked to support the project by asking management to assist the chosen employees by temporarily shifting a part of the employee's workload during the project.

The campaign proved to be a success. Although there were still employee availability problems from time to time, the project manager reported these problems to Ms. Kitchen, who would in turn contact the Division Vice President to assist in solving the problem. As a result, delays caused by lack of SMEs were greatly reduced, and the project ran on schedule to completion. A good communications strategy mitigated what could have been a serious risk to project completion.

Questions to Ask
When Bringing in Outside Expert

Q: What are your organization's processes for acquiring outside materials?

A:

Q: Do you deal with vendors directly or through a procurement department?

A:

Q: Does your organization have a preferred vendor list? If so, does it contain vendors that can fulfill your requirements?

Note: This question establishes whether the company has a preferred vendor list and, if they do, are the vendors appropriate given the requirements of the project.

A:

Q: How long is the process to establish a new vendor? How will it affect project planning and execution?

Note: This question relates to procurement activities and how long it takes to add a new vendor to a preferred vendor list. That timeline can impact project planning and execution.

A:

Q: How long does the established vendor process take? How will it affect project planning and execution?

A:

Q: Who will manage the vendor?

A:

may simply be less expensive to buy from a vendor whose expertise lies in producing what you need.

A few words about hiring vendors as contract workers: Organizations often hire vendors to do a significant portion of the work on a project. This usually happens when the work to be done is really outside of the organization's area of expertise. In many ways, hiring a vendor to assist can be less costly than hiring new employees and training them. We would offer several recommendations concerning hiring vendors:

- *Insist that the vendor participate in project planning with your team.* A "black box" project plan submitted from a vendor that has not participated in project planning should be suspect. You want your team to be familiar with all aspects of the project, including the vendor's role.

- *Be sure that the vendor specifies deliverables, dates, and costs in detail.* You want to know what you are receiving, when, and what it will cost you. Fixed-price contracts should be preferred over time and material contracts.

Be sure that change management is in place (we will cover this in Chapter 5). You want to be able to control costs by controlling changes that increase cost. The source of such changes may be the vendor, but it may also be internal to your organization. Be sure that it is very clear as to who may approve changes.

Project Plan

As mentioned previously, the project plan is a lot more than a series of tasks that are lined up by the project manager in a Gantt chart. Actually, the project plan includes all of the documentation we have discussed in this chapter. Before the development of many of the sophisticated project tools that are now available, the project manager would compile a project book containing all of the planning information. As the project progressed, the project manager would add status reports, risk reports, and many other pieces of information that were created by execution and controlling. At the end of the project, the project manager would add information from the lessons learned, and the project book would be archived so that it became an important resource for future projects.

Today, for smaller projects, this type of project book is still possible, although it may now consist of simple word processing documents. It may also consist of comprehensive project information residing in cyberspace using some of the sophisticated new tools that are available.

Now that we have completed our project planning, we will move on to project execution. Even so, you should now have a good understanding of why project planning is so important. If you have ever participated in a "Fire! Aim! Ready!" project, then you should already understand how project planning as we have explained it in this chapter can affect project success. In addition, you should now understand what sequence of activities is necessary to properly plan a project and how to use some basic project planning tools. Now, it's time to put our plan into action!

Summary

In this chapter, we've discussed primary and secondary project planning processes, showing how the primary processes form the core of planning while the secondary processes support the planning process. We have also reviewed the contents and structure of a project plan, highlighting the fact that the project plan contains all necessary documents of a project, not just a task list in a project tracking tool.

We also covered the work breakdown structure (WBS) and why it is crucial to project planning and how to create one down to the task level. Taking the tasks from a WBS, we showed how to define tasks and provided a template for task definitions. Then, using the tasks and their definitions, we created a network diagram that identifies the sequence of work to be done and the dependencies between tasks. Using this network diagram, we then created a project schedule and a critical path that reveals the actual duration of the project.

Finally, we explored three important supporting processes—quality planning, risk planning, and communication planning—and how to develop plans for dealing with each. Now, we're ready to execute our project!

Endnotes

1. *A Guide to the Project Management Body of Knowledge* (Newton Square, PA: Project Management Institute, 2000).

2. Ibid.

3. Harold Kerzner, Ph.D., *Project Management: A Systems Approach to Planning, Scheduling, and Controlling* (New York: John Wiley & Sons, 1998).

4. James P. Lewis, *The Project Manager's Desk Reference* (New York: McGraw-Hill, 1995).

5. See note 1.

6. Ibid.

7. Ibid.

8. Ibid.

CHAPTER 5

Project Execution and Control

After reading this chapter you will be able to

- Understand the difference between project plan execution and project control

- Appreciate why project control is one of the two keys to project success

- Be able to use project information to judge the health of a project

Definition of Project Execution and Project Control

A Guide to the Project Management Body of Knowledge[1] defines project execution as "coordinating people and other resources to carry out the (project) plan." This definition of project execution is deceptively simple; under the direction of the project manager, the project team, vendors, and others carry out the tasks that are defined in the project plan in order to produce the project deliverables. Would that the world was so simple! In reality, even smaller, less complex projects often experience untold problems.

That is why, as stated in the objectives, project control is one of the two keys to project success (the other, as previously covered, is project planning). Returning to our source, here is the definition of project control: "Ensuring that project objectives are met by monitoring and measuring progress regularly to identify plan variances so that corrective actions may be taken."[2]

To understand why project control is so important, let's use the analogy of an airplane flying toward a destination. The airplane is in perfect flying condition as it heads toward its destination; however, even on a perfectly clear day, wind currents in the air can push the airplane off course. As the pilot monitors the gauges, he or she will notice if the airplane is being pushed off course and compensate by steering the airplane back in the other direction, always heading toward its destination.

If you were to graph the airplane's path, it would not be a straight line, but more of a curve, first drifting in one direction and then the other, and constantly being steered back toward the proper destination. One of the purposes of project control is to provide the information on whether or not the airplane is off course, as well as the guidance to move it back on course.

The project manager is the pilot, always monitoring the gauges and ready to steer the project back on course. There is more to flying the airplane than just steering it. The pilot is always monitoring the systems, making sure that the plane has enough fuel to reach the destination, and making sure that all of the airplane's systems are functioning properly. If fuel runs short or if a system malfunctions, the pilot is there to decide what to do next. If something does go wrong, the pilot can decide what should be done to correct the problem.

So too, the project manager is at the controls, monitoring the project to ensure that if something goes wrong, the correct response is made. We have seen that airplanes are affected by other outside forces in addition to winds aloft. In the summer, storms are a great threat, and the pilot must steer carefully to avoid them. The same is true with projects: Outside forces beyond the project can threaten project success. Once again, the project manager is there to guide the project around or through such threats.

Project **Plan Execution**

Both project plan execution and project control consist of primary and secondary processes. In the case of project plan execution, the execution is the primary process and there are several secondary processes. The three most important secondary processes are work authorization, and information collection and distribution (see Exhibit 5.1).

Work Authorization

Work authorization is permission for work to begin on a task or phase of a project. The purpose of work authorization is to ensure that all prerequisites to the work at hand are complete and that resources are available to complete the work. Work authorization presupposes that information collection and distribution are also happening.

The source of authorization varies depending on the size and complexity of the project. In the case of an authorization for an individual

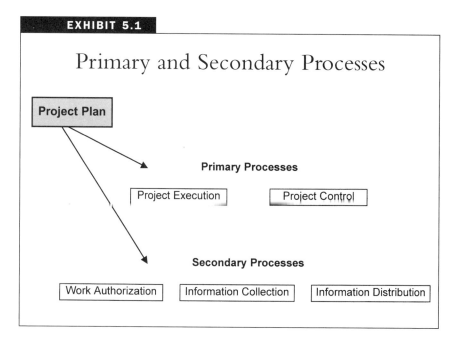

EXHIBIT 5.1

Primary and Secondary Processes

117

task, normally the project manager authorizes work to begin. In some projects, especially smaller ones, the project manager may do this informally, through conversation or an e-mail message. On larger projects, there may be a more formal procedure to follow. In the case of a large, complex project, there are often phase-gates (i.e., points at which the project is reevaluated to be sure that all is as it should be before continuing). The project may not pass the phase-gate without the authorization of a major stakeholder. Different types of software can be used to automate and track the work authorization process.

Information Collection

Information collection is the crucial element in both project plan execution and project control. Think back to the airplane example. If the airplane's navigation equipment malfunctions, and there is no information on the direction in which it is traveling, it becomes very difficult for the pilot to stay on course, particularly in bad weather. Occasional flights have ended in tragedy on a mountainside for lack of guidance in bad weather. A project is no different: Without information on progress and possible problems, a project can quickly go astray. As we have already seen, a project without a plan is a disaster waiting to happen. A project with a plan but no ongoing information is no less prone to a bad ending. Dead reckoning is as dangerous to a project as it is to flight.

What information should be collected about tasks? For guidance, let's return to the documents that were prepared in the project plan, in this case the task description. If we look at our project plan, the documents that immediately come to mind are the task description, the work breakdown structure (WBS), the quality plan, and the risk plan.

From the task description, we know the amount of effort that is required to complete the task. We also know when the task is supposed to be completed. Many people would then ask one of two questions:

118

(1) what percentage of the work is done? or (2) when will it be done? Beware that both of these questions have hidden traps.

In the former, you will most likely receive a positive answer indicating that most of the work is done. Perhaps it is human nature, but regardless of reality, most estimates seem to be about 80 percent finished, until the day that the task is due. This type of estimate will lead to faulty information later on, when we are using the information for project control purposes. The answer to the second question will usually be that the task will be done on time. However, when the day arrives, it is often not done.

Two basic questions will yield information that is needed to get to the true state of the project:(1) how many hours (or days, if you have described the effort in those terms) have the resources been working on the task? and (2) how many hours (days) will be needed to complete the task? These questions also presuppose another factor of project execution and control: You cannot study what you do not track. It is vital for project success that records are kept of all time that is spent on individual tasks. The answers to these two questions yield valuable information. By totaling the two answers, it is easy to find out if the task is taking more effort than expected, as well as come up with a prognosis on whether the task will be completed on time.

Before exploring this problem further, it should be noted that even if the project was going as originally predicted regarding time and progress, a project manager should normally seek additional information. Even though a particular task is done on time and within budget, there may be problems that are not yet apparent. There are additional questions to ask when the project is not turning out as planned regarding time and effort, such as (1) Was the level of effort calculated correctly? and (2) Was it based on experience, other inputs, or a guesstimate? These questions can also be linked with, were the resources assigned adequate? Did the resources have the level of technical expertise and knowledge to perform the task with the effort as estimated? The answers to all of these questions can affect the rest of the project. If other tasks were estimated similarly, will there be problems coming later on? We may also ask, was the task delayed because a task on which it depended was also late?

Let's turn to the WBS to search for other clues about project health. In the WBS, the level just above the task at hand is a description of the deliverable that the task takes part in producing. Asking questions about the intended deliverable in comparison with what the task is actually delivering will provide additional information about how the project is progressing. From Chapter 4, you will recall that the two questions asked about a deliverable were (1) what is it and (2) what does it do?

If we compare those answers with the deliverable from the task in question, we can see if there are any discrepancies. One of the culprits that can cause effort to increase on a task is gold plating, which is adding more to a deliverable than is required by the project specification. This is often a problem on client projects, where resources, with good intentions, seek to add value by doing more than is required. It is also a major source of effort overruns on many projects. You may also discover here that the problem is scope creep, where a project stakeholder has requested that additions be made without getting proper authorization (more on this when we talk about change control).

Before we finish with the information collection process, let's say a few words about the manner and timing of information collection. In smaller projects, the project manager may be able to collect information informally, through e-mails, memos, or direct conversation with project team members. On larger projects, this will not be possible.

Many software and Internet tools are available now to assist in data collection. Most of these tools are collaborative in nature, meaning that

TIPS & TECHNIQUES

Questions to Ask
When Tasks are Finished Late

Q: How many hours (or days, if you have described the effort in those terms) have the resources been working on the task?

A:

Q: How many hours (days) will be needed to complete the task?

A:

Q: Was the level of effort calculated correctly?

A:

Q: Was the estimate based on experience, other inputs, or a guesstimate?

A:

Q: Were the resources assigned adequate?

A:

Q: Did the resources have the level of technical expertise and knowledge to perform the task with the effort as estimated?

A:

Q: If other tasks were estimated in a similar manner, will there be problems later on? Was the task delayed because a task on which it depended was also late?

A:

individuals may enter the information themselves. Because these tools usually contain project information, the analysis of the information is automated.

At the same time, the project manager must ensure that information is entered and analyzed regularly. Weekly collection and analysis is the optimum alternative, but certainly no less frequently than every two weeks would be the minimum. Particularly in large, complex projects, problems have a way of growing exponentially when they are not found, reported, tracked, and solved efficiently and quickly.

Information Distribution

At the end of the project control section in this chapter, project status reporting is discussed in more detail because it is so closely linked to project control. In Chapter 4, communication planning is defined as "the process required to ensure timely and appropriate generation, collection, dissemination, storage, and ultimate disposition of project information."[3] Information distribution during project plan execution is the execution of the project communications plan. Carrying out the communications plan is a crucial factor in project success, in particular when it pertains to the project sponsor and other high-level stakeholders (see Exhibit 5.2).

In Chapter 2, when the STO (strategic, tactical, operational) model was introduced, it was emphasized that the real glue that holds the model together is communications. During project execution, two-way communications throughout all levels of the organization are vital. If project initiation and planning have been done properly, then the project will be in alignment with the firm's mission and goals. The project charter will communicate organizational strategy to the project team and other stakeholders. There must also be an appropriate communication back to the strategic level, in order to ensure that the executives of the organization are aware of what is happening.

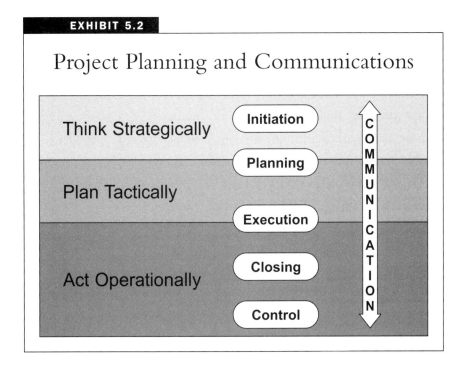

EXHIBIT 5.2

Project Planning and Communications

Think Strategically — Initiation

Plan Tactically — Planning

Execution

Act Operationally — Closing

Control

COMMUNICATION

We will talk about the appropriate level of detail during our discussion of project control, but we would like to point out a serious error that often occurs in firms, as well as with vendors. When problems are occurring in the depths of a project, often the problems are not known, because of a lack of project control or because the project team does not want to reveal them.

It may be understandable that the project team is unwilling to reveal bad news, given that in some organizations the bad news bearer is beaten up (not literally, of course). This may make the project manager reticent to give bad news. However, strategic and tactical managers need to know the bad news as early as possible, so they can react appropriately.

By reacting appropriately, we mean that strategic and tactical managers ought to find ways to support project teams and solve problems. A good example would be In the Real World, "Mitigating Risk with

Communications," in Chapter 4. The project team had identified that the most serious risk for completing the project on time and budget would be if the subject matter experts from the business areas did not have time to do the project work in addition to their own jobs.

In this case, the vice president of human resources, the project sponsor, had worked through the other functional vice presidents to identify and choose the resources. If a task was running behind because the subject matter expert lacked time, the project manager communicated with the vice president of human resources, requesting assistance for that person.

She in turn communicated with the functional vice president, requesting that they help the subject matter expert's supervisor to free the employee from other responsibilities in order to complete project work. The firm's communication plan, along with the participation of the project sponsor, helped it to successfully complete the project. The firm's experience can serve as a model for how good communications can support project success.

Project Control

In the case of project control, there is one primary process: project status reporting. There are five secondary processes: schedule control, change control, risk control, and quality assurance and control. These subprocesses all depend heavily on information collection and information distribution (see Exhibit 5.3).

Schedule Control and Earned Value

Schedule control consists of monitoring the project schedule to determine if the project is on schedule and making any necessary changes. The most important tool used in schedule control is earned value estimation.

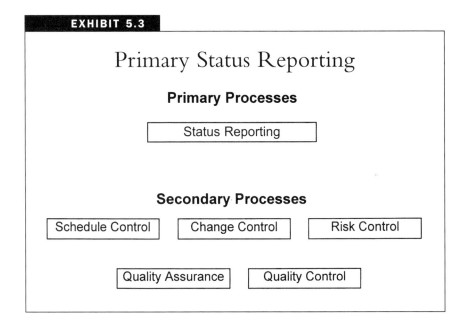

EXHIBIT 5.3

Primary Status Reporting

Primary Processes

Status Reporting

Secondary Processes

Schedule Control | Change Control | Risk Control

Quality Assurance | Quality Control

Earned value management is a technique used to integrate a project's scope, schedule, and resources and to measure and report project performance from initiation to close-out. As with critical path, it is a technique that is rarely done manually, but learning how earned value is calculated will be helpful in understanding the premise behind the earned value calculations and therefore the results of earned value. Exhibit 5.4 illustrates the key terms involved with calculating earned value.

To illustrate how earned value is calculated, let's take an example. Let us suppose that we have a task that is scheduled to be done by one person and will take 50 hours over the course of two weeks (Effort = 50 hours, Duration = 2 weeks). The effort will be evenly divided between the 2 weeks, 25 hours each.

At the end of the first week, the person performing the task reports that she actually worked on the task for 30 hours. This is not necessarily good news, as she indicates that she will probably have to work on the task for an additional 40 hours to complete the task. This means that,

| EXHIBIT 5.4 |

Earned Value Terms

Term	Acronym	Project Tracking Questions
Planned Value	PV	How much work should be done?
Earned Value	EV	How much work is really done?
Actual Cost	AC	How much did the work done really cost?
Budget at Completion	BAC	What is the total cost supposed to be when you are finished?
Estimate at Completion	EAC	Based on your current progress, what do you think the total costs will be at completion?
Cost Performance Index	CPI	What is the percentage of value for every dollar I spend?
Cost Variance	CV	How much is the budget behind or ahead of plan?
Schedule Performance Index	SPI	What is the percentage of progress rate compared to the original plan?
Schedule Variance	SV	How much is the schedule behind or ahead of plan?

in addition to some poor estimating, the resource has actually only completed about 43 percent of the work, or what should have taken roughly 21 hours. Here are the calculations that we would apply:

Planned Value (PV): 25	EV − PV = SV 21 − 25 = −4
Earned Value (EV): 21	$SPI = \frac{EV}{PV}$ $\frac{21}{25} = 84\%$

The Schedule Variance is a negative number, indicating that the project is behind schedule. The Schedule Performance Index of 84 percent tells that for every hour worked, we are getting only 50 minutes worth of value created.

These numbers actually tell us more than what appears at surface value. When a project does not use earned value and simply relies on completion date of tasks to calculate progress, a problem could arise. Suppose that the resource in this anecdote actually finished the task during week 2, and it did take an additional 20 hours. If only completion was tracked, it would seem that all is well. However, completion alone does not tell us what effect this problem had on other tasks. In total, the resource worked on the task for 20 hours more than planned. We must ask, why did this happen? Is it an isolated incident or is it a sign of other problems? What other tasks suffered because this one was over?

What if this project had 100 tasks and totaled around 4,000 hours. If only 10 percent of tasks were miscalculated in the same way, the project would be 514 hours over schedule and would have a good chance of coming in late. Tracking earned value for a schedule provides the additional information needed to understand what is really happening.

Let's take the same example now, only apply the cost factor. Let us say that the resource was an employee whose total cost was $100 per hour. Applying the proper calculations we find:

Planned Value (PV): $2500		
Actual Cost (AC) in dollars: $3000		
Earned Value (EV) $2100		

$$EV - PV = CV \qquad \$2500 - \$3000 = \$500$$

$$CPI - \frac{CV}{AC} \qquad \frac{\$2100}{\$3000} = 70\%$$

These calculations tell us that the task is over cost, $500 to be exact. The Cost Performance Index also tells us that for every dollar spent, only $.70 worth of value is being created. We can ask the same questions that we asked about running behind schedule. Although this is only one task over cost, here again, even if a small percentage of tasks are also over cost, the effect could be significant. To see how significant, we can apply the formula for Estimate at Completion, which calculates the end cost of the project based on the present results:

Budget at Completion (BAC): $400,000

Cost Performance Index (CPI): 70%

Estimate at Completion = $\frac{\text{BAC}}{\text{CPI}}$ = $\frac{\$400,000}{0.70}$ = $570,000 (approximately)

What we can see from the last set of figures is that this project will run over cost by more than $170,000, a serious cost overrun. Yet, if we do not calculate earned value and only track when tasks are completed, we risk not being aware of problems until much too late in the project, perhaps even just at completion.

Many organizations do not calculate earned value for their projects. One of the main reaons is that they don't plan projects, and it is very difficult to track something that is not planned. There are even organizations that plan, but do not collect the information necessary to do the calculations. Tracking resource hours and other expenses against the project schedule and calculating earned value will not guarantee that your projects will always be on time and on budget, but it will guarantee that if there are problems, you will be alerted much earlier on and have a better chance of correcting the problems.

Consider this example: A task is supposed to take one person 30 hours to complete over a two-week duration, about 15 hours each week. At the end of the first week, the resource has spent 22 hours and has about 18 hours left to work on the task. We now know that the task will take a total of 40 hours to complete, which is 33 percent more than allotted for in the task description. Although the task may be completed at the end of the second week (on time), we already know that if it takes the time as predicted, the task would be 33 percent over budget!

We must also consider that if work originally scheduled to take 15 hours actually took 22 hours, how do we know that the work predicted to take 18 hours will not take even longer? We actually don't know. We do know that now we must get to the root cause of the additional effort.

Based on earned value calculations, the schedule variance for this task at the end of the first week is -7 (hours), indicating by the negative number that the task is behind schedule (see Exhibit 5.5).

EXHIBIT 5.5

Earned Value and Potential Schedule Impact

Task A

Intended duration: 2 weeks
Effort: 30 hours (15 hours each week)

End of Week 1

Actual effort: 22 hours
Work accomplished: 15 hours
Work to finish: 18

Result

New task estimate: 40 hours = 33% greater than original
37.5 % of work is done instead of 50%
The task is behind schedule and is using too much resource time!

The Problem

Even if Task A is complete at the end of Week 2 (on time), it has used too much resource time!
Schedule variance = -7
Schedule variance index (SVI) = 68%
Every hour worked results in only 41 minutes of productive work time.

The Schedule Variance Index (SVI), a measure of productivity, is 68 percent. The best way to interpret the SVI is this: For every hour worked, the resource is accomplishing 68 percent, or roughly 40 minutes of work.

This task is seriously behind schedule. It is only one task, but the implications for the project are important. Some of the questions that should be asked at this point are: Why is this happening? What amount of effort will it take to complete the task? What will the effect be on the rest of the project?

We already know that it will take at least 10 additional hours to complete this task, so what are the implications to other similar tasks? What additional costs will the project incur as a result? According to the estimate in the task description, this task should cost $3,750 (30 hours x $125). We know that the actual cost at the end of the first week was $2,750 (22 hours x $125). We also know that the amount of work actually completed was 15 hours, so the earned value is $1,875 (15 hours x $125). We calculate the cost variance to be $875, which is over budget (see Exhibit 5.6).

The cost performance index, a measure of productivity, would then be $0.68. This means that for each dollar spent on this task, we have achieved a $0.68 return. It follows that this task is 32 percent over budget. It is just one task, but when you consider how many tasks there are in a project, having even a small percentage of tasks that are over budget in this way will cause a serious cost overrun. If we apply an estimate at completion calculation, we can see that the final cost of the task could be $5,515, rounded to the nearest dollar. This would be $1,765 dollars over budget.

You can see here why it is important to track hours and cost for each task. If all we looked at for this task was the completion by a certain date, which in this case probably would be met, we miss the fact that this task was seriously over budget.

EXHIBIT 5.6

Calculating the Cost Performance Index

Task A

Resource cost: $125 an hour
Estimated cost: $125 x 30 = $3750
First week estimated cost: $1875

End of Week 1

Actual cost: $125 x 22 = $2750
Cost overrun: $875

Result

New cost estimate: $125 x 40 = $5000
Cost overrun: $1250

The Problem

Even if Task A is complete at the end of Week 2 (on time),
there is a cost variance of $–875.
Cost performance index (CPI) = 68%
Every dollar spent creates only $0.68 of value.

Once you have determined that a variance exists in project schedule or cost, why it has happened, and what the solution is, a change must be made in the project schedule. Depending on the level of detail a project is using, this may be done through a schedule change control process or simply by using the project's change control process.

Before making the changes, all of the implications, in particular to overall schedule and cost, must be calculated. Approval of such a change will be made at the appropriate level of authority, depending on the cost of the change.

Change Control

Rare is the project that does not undergo any changes at all during its full cycle. Projects deal with change, and they are the subjects of frequent change. Change in a project is not bad, but uncontrolled and undocumented change has been the death of many a project. A well-planned project that is not properly controlled will run astray at some point. Change control does not mean that there cannot be any change, but that change must be regulated with a process to ensure that only those changes that will benefit the project's objectives happen.

Although the project manager is usually the person to manage change control in a project, he or she may not be the final decision maker on making a specific change. For example, a firm was developing software to automate several business processes that spanned several different computer programs. The new software would integrate the programs, meaning that employees would no longer have to print paper from one program in order to input information into another program.

At the same time, there are several points in the business process where an individual would have to input additional information through the new program. The project was properly initiated and planned, the specifications were completed, and the team was executing the tasks to produce the software. At this point, changes began to creep in from several different sources, threatening to overwhelm the project.

The first changes came from inside the project team. The team had several outstanding and creative programmers, and they found several ways that they felt they could enhance the program beyond what the business wanted for the end users. They began to code some of these changes, so that when the project status was reported at the proper interval, tasks were not completed on time and were running over budget. This is what is known as gold plating and can be a serious problem if not controlled.

When the project manager discovered the changes, he did several things: First, he stopped the programmers from coding any other changes from the original specifications. Then he had the programmers write up the changes they were proposing, along with estimates of the additional effort and cost that would result. These were then proposed as changes to the project sponsor.

The project sponsor and any other stakeholder in the project must decide whether the changes are worth the additional effort and cost. They must also decide if the changes are acceptable in light of what effect they may have on the rest of the project. The project manager must also report on what the effect of the extra work will be in case the changes are not accepted. There may be extra expense for rework if the changes must be undone. If the project were being done for an outside client, this situation could seriously affect the project's overall profitability.

Changes in project scope do not always start from the inside, either. Frequently, the project stakeholders ask for changes. Using the same example, it is quite possible that a stakeholder (e.g., a client) wants changes made to the proposed system. Curiously, stakeholders seldom make the connection between these kinds of changes and the additional effort and cost they require.

A change control process prevents changes from drowning the project. The change control process documents all requested changes so that the project team can determine what effect the changes will have in terms of effort and cost. Once the estimates are complete, the stakeholder can accept or reject the change. The key here is that the project manager must have the authority to refuse any change if the stakeholder does not sign off on the effects of the change on the project, either on the cost, the resources needed, or the delivery date.

As mentioned in Chapter 3, the Iron Triangle operates in any situation of change. The three sides of the triangle represent time, cost, and performance, as shown in Exhibit 5.7. A change to any one element will necessitate a change to one or both of the others. If the project manager does not control one of the three sides, then he or she is not really managing the project.

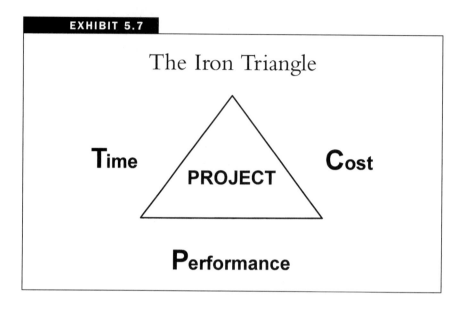

EXHIBIT 5.7

The Iron Triangle

Time

PROJECT

Cost

Performance

The change control process need not be complex. It can be as simple as a change control request and a change control log. Many different software tools are also available to assist in change control.

Risk Control

Risk control has several facets: (1) monitoring project results for signs that risks may occur or may have occurred, (2) reviewing risk responses that have been taken to see if they were effective, (3) reviewing project goals and objectives to ensure that they are still valid, and (4) reviewing the project context to see if any changes in external factors may affect the project.

As with all of the other categories of project control, risk control relies on a well-constructed risk plan along with proper execution of the plan. In practical terms, risk monitoring also depends on information gathering to find the information needed to determine whether any risks are either imminent or actually happening.

When gathering and reviewing project information, the project manager must also constantly refer to the risk plan, which contains information about possible risks, the warning signs that they may happen, and how the risks will be dealt with if they happen. Once the signs of risk appear, the project manager initiates the risk response plan and continues to monitor the situation. Finally, the project manager evaluates the effectiveness of the response to determine if changes need to be made in the risk plan.

Quality Assurance and Control

In essence, quality is divided into two facets: quality assurance and quality control. These terms are often confused. In the context of project management, quality assurance refers to project management and quality control refers to the product or service that the project is producing. Quality assurance refers to all of the various activities that are a part of the project's quality.

The project manager monitors quality tasks in the same manner that all other project tasks are monitored: Are they happening on schedule and according to plan? Are quality tasks completed within their allocations of effort and cost? If the project quality tasks are completed satisfactorily

TIPS & TECHNIQUES

Quality Assurance versus Quality Control

Quality Assurance

Monitor project execution to see that all project tasks are carried out according to the project plan in order to ensure quality.

Quality Control

Determine that a particular deliverable meets the quality standards that are set for it.

according to plan, it is not an absolute guarantee that quality will be up to par, but it is an indication that there is a better chance that quality will be present.

Quality control consists of the various tasks within the quality plan that determine whether the actual product of the project meets the quality standards that have been established for it. At times, a general quality standard, such as International Standards Organization (ISO), or a more specific standard, such as regulation by the Food and Drug Administration (FDA) in the pharmaceutical industry, is required. At other times, the project team sets the quality standard during the planning process.

In either case, the project manager, along with any quality professionals who might be involved, are responsible for ensuring that the quality standards are met. The importance of quality assurance is that it attempts to ensure that quality is in place before anything is produced, whereas quality control is more focused on testing the results to see that quality standards have been achieved. When quality assurance functions well, it is less likely that there will be problems with quality. When quality control does find that quality standards have not been met, there is usually increased cost for rework.

Status Reporting

Status reporting is the activity that conveys information about project progress to individuals or groups that require information. Status reporting should happen frequently; we would suggest that status reporting should happen on a weekly basis or at least once every two weeks. Leaving longer intervals than two weeks creates a risk that problems that occur may go unnoticed and uncorrected for too long a period. This correlates well with the basic duration of a project task—no more than two weeks.

The project manager is primarily responsible for status reporting, although on larger, more complex projects, an administrator or project administrator may collect information and report status to the overall project manager, who would then report to other stakeholders as is necessary.

The project status report should be concise and to the point. Depending on the audience, it may have a greater or lesser level of detail. For the project sponsor and anyone else who has a direct stake in the project (including the project team), the status report should be detailed enough so that the project sponsor or other decision-making stakeholder will have sufficient information to understand the state of the project and be able to make decisions concerning the project. If some issues are more complex, other documents explaining the issue may accompany the status report, which should include the following:

- A list of tasks completed during the period
- A list of tasks that should have been completed during the period and were not (including those that should have been started and were not)
- A list of tasks in progress as of the date of the status report
- The lists of tasks may be output from any project tracking software that is used.
- Earned value calculations should be included. If they indicate any problems, any information concerning root causes should be included.
- The status report should contain a list of issues that have arisen, along with any detailed information about the issues.

Status reports that are intended for other audiences may have different levels of detail and may not include all of the information indicated here. The project manager can take guidance from the project communications plan as to the content and format of reports to different

EXHIBIT 5.8

Project Status Report

Date:	Project Title:

Project Description:

Status:

Reporting Period:

Activities Performed During this Reporting Period:

Activities Planned for Next Reporting Period:

Issues/Resolutions Activity:

Project Change Activity:

Problems, Concerns, Recommendations:

Additional Comments:

groups. The model status report in Exhibit 5.8 is also included in the URL that accompanies this book.

Project Closing

Project closing, the final phase of a project, is very important to both the project at hand and future projects. Project closing consists of two activities: contract close-out and administrative close-out.[4] Contract close-out is of particular importance when the project is for a client, because this is the process by which the client formally accepts the project deliverables (usually with a written document). Even when a project is done internally in a firm, it is a good idea to have a major stakeholder sign off on project completion. Project close-out also applies to when project budgets and spending are finalized, so that actual project cost can be determined. Again, for a client situation, finalizing budget and spending correctly can be the difference between a profitable project and a money-losing project.

The other aspect of project closing is administrative close-out. Administrative close-out is of particular importance for future projects; it includes documenting all of the project information in an archive, including lessons learned. All of the information that has been kept about a project becomes a rich source for future projects. For example, during project planning, it is often difficult to estimate the effort required to complete different tasks. When the project team is able to consult with the estimates and the actual effort is recorded for those tasks, it becomes possible to estimate with greater accuracy.

When developing a risk plan, it is also very useful to consult with the lessons learned of previous projects—good and bad—as well as the risk plan and status reports of previous projects. As these records accumulate, firms can use the records to begin to create best practices in project management that will benefit the entire firm.

Roles in Project Execution and Closing

So far during this chapter, we have been chiefly focused on the project manager's role. There is no doubt that the project manager's expertise can make or break a project. In addition, the technical and subject matter expertise of the rest of the team are essential to project success. At this point, many senior managers and executives may sit back and say, "Let them go to it, this is really not my area to be involved." But nothing could be farther from the truth!

The active involvement of senior executives and managers in strategic projects is extremely important. The following is a list of suggestions for how senior executives and managers can help promote the welfare of projects in their organization:

- *Do promote communication.* Communication is the lifeblood of projects in any organization. For various reasons, communication between levels and different functional areas is often difficult. You can foster communication by letting various groups within the organization know that you find this project important. Insist on receiving timely communications from the project team in order to understand what is really happening.

- *Don't punish the message bearer.* Too often, when a project manager has bad news to report, he or she takes the brunt of the bad emotion that this news creates. Project managers will then hesitate to bring bad news to executives, making it more difficult for them to get problems solved.

- *Do get involved in planning.* Although it is not a good use of your time to get involved in the detailed planning of strategic projects, it is very useful for you to ensure that the information in the project charter accurately reflects the correct business needs to support the firm's strategic objectives.

- *Don't shuffle priorities.* We often hear project managers complain that the highest-priority project belongs to the last person who speaks to...whoever (think of the story in Chapter 1). Snap decisions on changing priorities based on an individual complaint can wreak havoc on more than just one project.

- *Do decide on priorities.* There are times when priorities change. It is important that the decisions around changing priorities are made known to all concerned and are communicated in a timely fashion. Involving project managers in decisions will often help in finding creative solutions to resource shortages.

- *Don't ask for miracles.* Project managers are not magicians, and they are prone to develop ulcers when asked to achieve the impossible. Good project planning with competent estimates around resources and effort yield project end dates that are achievable.

TIPS & TECHNIQUES

Project Management Dos and Don'ts

DO

- Promote communication.
- Decide on priorities.
- Get involved in planning.

DON'T

- Punish the message bearer.
- Shuffle priorities.
- Ask for miracles.

Summary

Project execution and, in particular, project control are the heart of the project management life cycle. Project control is one of the two keys to project success (the other being project planning).

Many different sources quote the success rate of projects as being somewhere between 25 and 30 percent. What that means is that only 25 or 30 projects out of 100 will be completed on time, on budget, and deliver a quality deliverable that will be used as intended. By implementing proper project methodology, any firm can be among the 25 to 30 percent of projects that succeed. Remember that projects are the strategic lifeblood of an organization. Understanding and promoting strategic project management in an organization goes a long way toward fostering long-term success.

Endnotes

1. *A Guide to the Project Management Body of Knowledge* (Newton Square, PA: Project Management Institute, 2000).

2. Ibid.

3. Ibid.

4. Ibid.

CHAPTER 6

Project Management Maturity

After reading this chapter you will be able to

- Describe what project management maturity is

- Understand the levels of project management maturity

- Understand several project management maturity models that are available today

- Identify how the STO model integrates with project management maturity

Project Management Maturity Models

In practicing project management, some organizations are farther ahead in defining, following, and implementing the processes, inputs, outputs, tools, and techniques than others. In this chapter, we define what project management maturity is and review one well-known project management maturity model and another new model proposed by the Project Management Institute (PMI). We also identify how the STO (strategic, tactical, operational) solution model integrates with the levels of project management maturity.

First, let's take a look at the definition of maturity. Webster's defines *maturity* as "the quality state of being mature; full development." When you think of project management maturity, think about past projects you've been involved in, either as a sponsor or a key stakeholder. You probably have a sense of how well-developed your company is related to project management maturity, but you haven't had a model on which to understand what still needs to happen in your organization for project management to become part of the fabric of your culture. To gain more insight about where you believe your organization currently is, take a few minutes now and complete the self-assessment on indicators of project management maturity in Tips and Techniques, "Project Maturity Questions."

Did you finish? Great! Now how many times did you check "It Depends?" Certainly one of the components that makes project management such a great strategic tool is consistent, repeatable documented processes and historical information. "It Depends" is an answer for individuals and organizations who do not want to look closely at continuous process improvement.

Although many maturity models exist and more are being created as we finish writing this book, there are two primary project management maturity models we'll review here.

The first maturity model we'll take a look at is the one created by Project Management Solutions, Inc.[1] They have developed a project management maturity model that uses five levels of maturity and examines an organization's implementation of project management across the nine knowledge areas of *A Guide to the Project Management Body of Knowledge* (PMBOK). The five levels of project management maturity in organizations as described by Project Management Solutions, Inc. are as follows:

Level 1: Initial Process

- Ad-hoc processes
- Management awareness

Level 2: Structure Process and Standards

- Basic process, not standard on all projects, used on large, highly visible projects

144

- Management supports and encourages
- Mix of intermediary and summary-level information
- Estimates, schedules based on expert knowledge and generic tools
- Mostly a project-centric focus

TIPS & TECHNIQUES

Project Maturity Questions

Questions	Yes	No	It Depends
We have a lot of ad-hoc process.	☐	☐	☐
We have basic processes we use on mostly large, highly visible processes.	☐	☐	☐
Our management encourages and supports project management.	☐	☐	☐
Project estimates and schedules are based on expert knowledge and generic tools.	☐	☐	☐
Project processes are integrated with corporate process.	☐	☐	☐
Our project processes are standardized and repeatable.	☐	☐	☐
Management mandates project management compliance.	☐	☐	☐
Project estimates and schedules are normally based on organization specifics.	☐	☐	☐
Processes are in place to measure project effectiveness and efficiency.	☐	☐	☐
Management focuses on continuous improvement.	☐	☐	☐

Level 3: Organizational Standards and Institutionalized Process

- All process standard for all projects, repeatable
- Management has institutionalized processes
- Summary and detailed information
- Baseline and informal collection of actuals
- Estimates, schedules may be based on industry standards and organizational specifics

Level 4: Managed Process

- Processes integrated with corporate processes
- Management mandates compliance
- Management takes an organizational entity view
- Solid analysis of project performance
- Estimates, schedules are normally based on organization specifics
- Management uses data to make decisions

Level 5: Optimizing Process

- Processes to measure project effectiveness and efficiency
- Processes in place to improve project performance
- Management focuses on continuous improvement

This model then takes the nine knowledge areas of the PMBOK and describes the components of each knowledge area and the levels of maturity for each component. Let's look at an example of maturity levels 1 to 5 for project scope management.

- *Level 1.* A statement of scope is prepared on a project. However, the format and content of this statement are ad hoc—no standards exist for such and each one looks different.
- *Level 2.* A clearly defined and documented process describing the preparation of project charters and scope statements,

which is enforced by organizational management for larger, more visible projects. Projects are consistently started with the defined project charter; scope statements are consistently prepared in accordance with the defined process and format.

- *Level 3.* Project assumptions and constraints are clearly documented in the scope statement. A statement of work is created for each project with specific definition of the work and is approved by organizational management. The project scope is regularly determined and documented by a fully integrated project team, including the business unit, technical groups, strategic groups as necessary, the client, and so on.

- *Level 4.* Scope, assumptions, constraints, and interproject dependencies are thoroughly documented and activity monitored and managed throughout the project.

- *Level 5.* The process of determining and documenting scope is regularly examined to ascertain process improvements. Experience data from a project repository are regularly used to improve on standard templates for scoping and the development of requirements. Scope is regularly monitored, and projected deviations from scope are foreseen and carefully documented.

Finally, this model also identifies a special-interest component within each level—the project office. In Chapter 7, we discuss the project management office in detail, because it is a tool that can help you with some of the strategic decisions you need to make, if it is positioned at the right level in your organization.

So what does project management maturity mean to you? Well, if you are trying to establish project management as a way of doing business in your organization, recognizing the characteristics of each level will help you identify what needs to be done to lay the proper foundation within the organization and why you may be encountering obstacles you hadn't anticipated. In the Real World, "It's Not Just a Training Issue" illustrates how to identify the problem, and not solve it!

The OPM3™ Project Management Maturity Model[2]

The PMI has recently issued a new standard for project management maturity, called OPM3™. This new standard, the second one we will consider,

IN THE REAL WORLD

It's Not Just a Training Issue

The IT department staff of a major consumer packaged goods manufacturer realized that they had reached a critical point in their organization and needed to implement standardized processes around how they managed their IT projects. In addition to documenting all of their processes, the CIO wanted to ensure that everyone in his area who would be involved on a project spoke the same language and understood the same principles of project management.

The CIO mandated that everyone, regardless of level of experience, would receive training on how to manage a project. A well-known vendor was chosen, and training on standard project management was rolled out nationally and internationally. In addition, a Web-based project management tool was implemented so that virtual teams could be easily put together to manage global projects.

Despite all of this effort, this organization was still at Level 2 project management maturity because the rest of the organization never adopted the IT project management standards. The need for project management was seen primarily as a tactical IT function rather than as a strategic tool to be used throughout the organization. This is just one typical example of how difficult it is to achieve project management maturity throughout an organization. Also, complicating matters even more is the fact that there may be different functional areas operating under different levels of project maturity within a single organization.

has been several years in the making and represents a significant step on the part of the organization. Because the standard is new, we briefly review its components here. We believe that many organizations will begin to utilize this standard, so that within a few years, a body of information will be available on the implementation of this new standard.

OPM3 is a three-dimensional model that correlates project management, program management, and portfolio management across an organization (see Exhibit 6.1). The first dimension of the model uses the stages of process improvement: standardize, measure, control, and improve. Each of these stages can be correlated to a continuum of progress toward project management maturity. The second dimension of the model consists of project management, program management, and portfolio management. The third dimension of the model, which really holds the whole model together, is the sequence of project management processes as originally defined by the PMI: initiating, planning, executing, controlling, and closing.

Underneath the three-dimensional model of OPM3 is a system for measuring project management maturity that is based on the collective experience of many project management professionals, which the PMI has been collecting for some time. The PMI has determined the following:[3]

- Best practices associated with organizational project management
- Capabilities that are prerequisites or that aggregate to Each Best Practice
- The Observable Outcomes that signify the existence of a given Capability in the organization
- Key Performance Indicators (KPIs) and Metrics that provide the means to measure Outcomes
- The Pathways that identify the Capabilities aggregating to the Best Practices being reviewed.

EXHIBIT 6.1

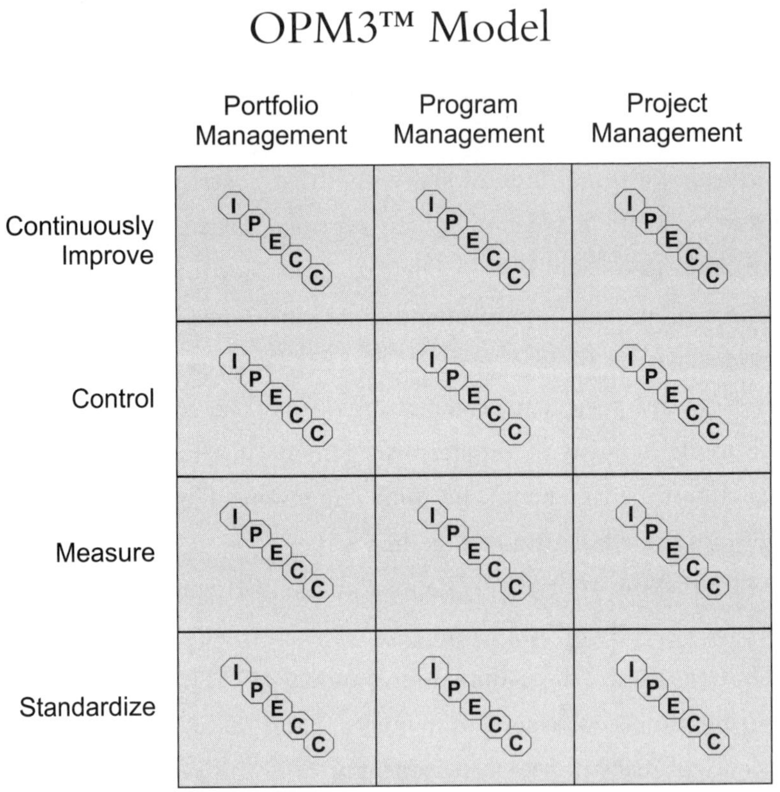

OPM3™ Model

	Portfolio Management	Program Management	Project Management
Continuously Improve	I P E C C	I P E C C	I P E C C
Control	I P E C C	I P E C C	I P E C C
Measure	I P E C C	I P E C C	I P E C C
Standardize	I P E C C	I P E C C	I P E C C

Source: Adapted from Project Management Institute's Project Management Maturity Model (OPM3™), a paper presented by Steve Fahrenkrog, PMP; Fred Abrams, PMP; William B. Haeck, PMP; and David Whelbourn, MBA at the PMI North American Congress 2003.

OPM3 provides a database containing best practices in the areas of project management, portfolio management, and program management—the constituent parts of organizational project management—as well as the road map to assess and improve the organization's maturity.

The model is based on identifying key performance indicators (KPIs) in an organization. The indicators are evidence of measurable outcomes, whose existence is confirmation of a particular capability.

When all of the capabilities are achieved in a best practice, the organization has put in place a building block on the way to maturity. As the building blocks are put into place in each area of organizational project management (i.e., project management, portfolio management, and program management), then the organization rises through the stages of process improvement: standardize, measure, control, and continuously improve. OPM3 presupposes that the entire process is carried out using the PMI standard.

Because the new PMI standard for project management maturity has just been released, it will be interesting to follow the progress of different organizations that implement the new standard.

The STO Solution Model

Throughout this book, we've referred to the STO model of project management that we use. We have also offered the opinion that executives usually view project management as more of an operational tool rather than a strategic or tactical tool. Exhibit 6.2 describes how the STO model interacts with the maturity model we've presented.

The arrows represent the flow of information between the levels of the STO solution model and between the STO model and the levels of project management maturity within an organization. Let's look at the three components of the STO solution model and how they interact with the five levels of project management maturity.

Operational

The operational level of project management is where you typically find a lot of ad-hoc processes within the functional departments and a general recognition that there is something called project management that will help implement the various functional and organizational initiatives a department is usually tasked with completing.

151

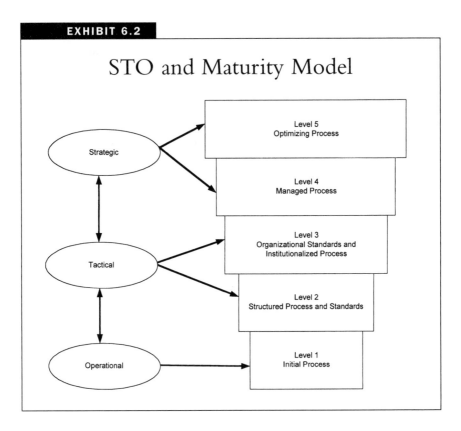

EXHIBIT 6.2

STO and Maturity Model

Level 5
Optimizing Process

Level 4
Managed Process

Level 3
Organizational Standards and
Institutionalized Process

Level 2
Structured Process and Standards

Level 1
Initial Process

Strategic

Tactical

Operational

Typically, each functional area may have its own tools for managing projects and, although the teams may cross functions, the work generally gets done by people within the functional area or as a quid pro quo with another area. Changes to the project also happen on an ad-hoc basis and usually are not monitored or tracked.

Tactical

Let's look at Level 2 maturity first. As we've indicated previously, projects from a tactical standpoint in an organization usually do involve cross-functional teams working together, but the project manager is usually a talented technical lead or subject matter expert in one of the functional areas rather than a project manager coming out of a project management office.

In this scenario, documented processes and standards are in place for project management. These processes and standards involve how to develop a project plan, including work breakdown structure, project charter, scope statement, resource staffing, and so on. Formalized reporting on the status of the project is in place, and there is a documented method of change control for the project.

At this level, there is also a system that gathers, synthesizes, and organizes project information. For highly visible projects in larger organizations, a basic project office may be established, or this may be one of the roles of the project manager for smaller organizations.

An organization that exhibits Level 3 project management maturity would continue to develop and document more project management processes and standards. The project plan becomes more detailed in terms of cost and schedule baselines, as well as risks and risk response strategies. Project plans are updated to reflect change requests. Reports will include variance and performance measurement analysis and will expand to include information from other project areas such as risk, quality, human resources, and procurement.

At this level of maturity, change control of a project may be managed by a formalized entity such as a steering committee and will include formal processes of managing, monitoring, and tracking change requests. There may also be a centralized information system using an enterprise-wide tool to gather information and report project-related data. A project management office at this level is recognized by management as being the central point of project management methods and is integrated into the organization.

Strategic

The differences between Level 4 and Level 5 can be summed up in a few words—continuous improvement. Level 4 maturity evolves so that all processes are in place, in use, and integrated into other enterprise-wide processes. Level 5 basically focuses on how those project management processes and documentation can be improved by looking at them on a project-by-project basis and documenting lessons learned.

With Level 4 and Level 5 maturity, organizations typically have a program management office that resides at the executive level and examines all projects across the organization and ranks and rates their priority to the larger mission, goals, and objectives of the business and the potential impact of shareholder value. This is why we have been adamant about the strategic role that project management plays in organizations. If you take away only one crucial point from this book, let it be this: *If your projects are not aligned to the strategic goals of your organization, you are wasting time, money, and valuable resources, and your shareholders will notice eventually.*

Summary

In this chapter, we have discussed the meaning of project management maturity and looked at a common maturity model. We have also identified how the STO solution model integrates with the five levels of project management maturity. In the next chapter, we delve more deeply into the project management office and how it can help you align your projects to your business strategies.

Endnotes

1. J. Kent Crawford, *Project Management Maturity Model* (New York: Marcel Dekker, 2001).

2. Project Management Institute's Project Management Maturity Model (OPM3™), a paper presented by Steve Fahrenkrog, PMP; Fred Abrams, PMP; William B. Haeck, PMP; and David Whelbourn, MBA, at the PMI North American Congress, 2003.

3. Ibid.

CHAPTER 7

The Project Management Office

After reading this chapter you will be able to

- Understand why a project management office can take so many different forms

- Understand how a firm's structure affects the project management office

- Understand how the STO model affects the project management office

- Identify the characteristics for a project management office for any area within your firm

The Project Management Office

In the last few years, project management offices have become a very popular cure for firms' project management ills. Many firms decide to implement a project management office or project office without asking several fundamental questions. Project management offices also carry a variety of names; hereafter in this text, we refer to the entity as a PMO.

You might want to start by asking what the PMO will do. However, the answer to that question depends on other factors. Among these factors are: (1) what type of organization does the firm have (i.e., functional, matrix, projectized); (2) at what level in the organization will the project

155

office be located (i.e., strategic, tactical, operational); and (3) what level of project management maturity already exists within the organization?

Other questions that must be asked refer to the role of the PMO: will it merely provide administrative support to project operations, be a center of excellence for project management practitioners, be the managerial center to which project professionals report, or have complete responsibility for the planning and delivery of entire projects? All of these questions have a bearing on what a PMO will look like and how it will function.

A common error that firms make is to confuse the opening of a PMO with the implementation of project management in their firm. The two may happen simultaneously, but they are not the same. Implementing project management at a firm means beginning to use a sound, repeatable project methodology at some level in the organization with the objective of growing the methodology's use throughout the firm over a period of time. Creating a PMO means instituting an administrative, knowledge-based, tactical or strategic entity that will support project processes in a designated area and level of the firm.

If a firm is instituting project management for the first time in one area of a functional organization, a small project office that assists with administrative work, such as collecting information for status reporting or tracking change requests, could be helpful. A full-blown strategic project office would be overkill. Like implementing project management, implementing a project office is a project in itself, requiring each of the phases of project management that we have already covered earlier in this book.

How then can we describe the various forms that a PMO may take in a systematic way? If we look back at previous chapters in this book, we have covered a series of topics that can help determine the form that a PMO may take and how it might function. Those tools are an organizational structure analysis, the STO model, and the level of project management maturity of the organization. Exhibit 7.1 is a matrix that illustrates the different types of PMOs that are possible using organizational structural analysis and the STO model. We will use this matrix as a framework to analyze the different types of PMOs. As we discuss each type of office, we will also use project management maturity to help describe each office type's characteristics. Let's start by looking at the four orientations that a PMO may take.

Administrative-Support PMO

The administrative-support PMO provides different types of assistance to the project manager and the project. This type of PMO may assist in creating and updating the different sorts of documentation that are required depending on the project phase. This could include the project charter, any or all of the documents contained in the project plan (e.g., work breakdown structure, network diagram, risk, quality and communications plan).

The administrative-support PMO will have expertise in using the firm's chosen software tool to track the project. During project execution and control, the PMO may coordinate work authorization or issue the work authorization notices under the direction of the project manager. The PMO may handle change control documentation. It may collect individual status reports and consolidate them for the project manager, as well as collect hours and calculate earned value.

The administrative support PMO could have a role in collecting other types of documentation that are related to the project, but not specifically project documentation (e.g., specifications or work product). At project closing, the administrative-support PMO may ensure that all documents that require signoff have been received, final budgets are turned in, and all project documentation is properly formatted and archived. In

EXHIBIT 7.1

PMO Type Matrix

Administrative-Support	Center of Excellence	Managerial PMO	Delivery PMO
• Creates and updates project plan documentation during different project phases	• Serves as reference and resource center for project teams	• Serves as "home base" for project managers	• Responsible for delivering projects
• Uses expertise in the firm's chosen software tool to assist in tracking the project	• Supports individual project managers and teams during project phases	• Provides human resources support for project managers	• During a project, the project manager and team may report to the project manager to the PMO
• Coordinates work authorization	• Provides project management education	• Oversees project management career path from a management perspective	• Project manager represents the PMO to the organization
• Handles change control documentation	• Members serve as project consultants		
• Collects individual status information	• Members serve as consultants to upgrade project methodology		
• Compiles and disseminates status reports	• Establishes and maintains best practices		
• Collects progress information and calculates earned value	• Establishes and maintains project toolkit		
• Coordinates contract closeout	• Maintains library of project management books, periodicals, and other material		
• Assists with other project documentation	• Establishes and maintains project management career path information and programs		

Note: A single PMO will often have characteristics of several different PMO types, which are not mutually exclusive.

sum, the administrative-support PMO may do any administrative task necessary to support the project.

Center of Excellence PMO

The center of excellence PMO serves as a reference and resource for project teams. The members of this type of PMO would not be project managers, in the sense that they would not serve as project managers on individual projects, but they would have the more general role of supporting project management to the firm.

They may offer different types of education to members of the firm, assisting them in gaining knowledge about project management. They might also serve as project consultants, assisting the members of any project team with different facets of project management. For example, they could be available to assist a newer project manager during a project planning session or to help calculate and interpret earned value.

In some cases, where an organization is working to upgrade the quality of project management or a newly revised methodology, the members of a center of excellence PMO may be in charge of the effort (in which case, they would be the project managers of the improvement project). The center of excellence PMO would also work on establishing and maintaining best practices for project management that project teams could consult, as well as a library (virtual or otherwise) of books and other materials that could be consulted as necessary.

In sum, the center of excellence supports project management through knowledge and skill development.

Managerial PMO

A managerial PMO constitutes home base for project managers in an organization. Project managers would report to the PMO and receive all of their human resources support (e.g., payroll, benefits, evaluations) from the PMO. When project managers are assigned to projects, they would have an indirect (or dotted) line between them and the project sponsor and a direct (or solid) line between them and the manager or director of the PMO. The managerial PMO would also be concerned with the knowledge and skills of the project managers, but would not necessarily serve as a center of excellence.

Delivery PMO

The delivery PMO is actually responsible for delivering complete projects. The project managers and teams would not necessarily report to this PMO in the same way that they report to a managerial PMO, but for the duration of the project, the team would report to the project manager on an indirect basis and the project manager to the appropriate level within the PMO. The delivery PMO would have complete responsibility for the entire project and would relate to the rest of the firm in much the same way as a vendor relates to a client.

The project sponsor will probably be from the organization outside of the PMO, and the project manager would be the PMO representative who works directly with the project sponsor. Using the delivery PMO model, project teams would come together for the duration of the project and would either return to their functional areas after a project or simply be assigned to a new project. It would not be unusual to see project managers and other team members working on more than one project at a time.

Needless to say, in the real world, it is rare that a PMO has one single function, often combining some or all of these elements. How those elements come together also depends on the type of organization and the level in the organization at which the PMO is situated. Let's take a look at the various possibilities. Please note: If you have a good feel for your organization's type, you may want to skip ahead to the section that deals with that type.

Functional Organization

As you will recall from our discussion in Chapter 2, a functional organization is usually set up in silos, with little communication occurring among functional areas. There are direct lines of authority in each area, and most communication is vertical. Although it is possible to conduct proper project management in a functional organization, it is also the most challenging structure in which to do so (see Exhibit 7.2).

Operational Level

Because the project team is drawn from the ranks of employees with jobs, it is difficult for team members to perform their tasks and do their jobs at the same time. The project manager tends to be more of a coordinator than anything else, and the project sponsor must work very hard to ensure adequate communication among the functional areas to keep the project on track. Chances are good that this organization is very low on the project maturity scale.

EXHIBIT 7.2

Likelihood that PMO Characteristics Exist in a Functional Organization

STO LEVEL	Likelihood that PMO Characteristics Exist in a Functional Organization			
	Administrative-Support	Center of Excellence	Managerial PMO	Delivery PMO
Operational	✓	⇔	⇔	✗
Tactical	⇔	✗	⇔	✗
Strategic	⇔	✗	✗	✗

Legend: ✓ Very likely exists   ⇔ Somewhat likely exists   ✗ Not likely exists

A PMO at this level in a functional organization will most likely have the characteristics of an administrative-support PMO. It is very possible that it would consist of either the project manager or another person(s) who may be borrowed from other departments in the organization. This PMO will be successful if it can support the project within the confines of the possible, in particular by focusing on the identified areas of difficulty. For example, most, if not all, project team members have full-time jobs other than the project. The PMO can support team members by taking as much administrative work off their hands as possible. This could include documenting progress, collecting information for status reports, and tracking task startup and completion.

The PMO could greatly assist the project sponsor by seeing that project information is properly formatted and can be forwarded to stakeholders in different functional areas. This will help with cross-functional communication and may help keep the project on track. It is unlikely that any other type of PMO would be present at this level in a functional organization.

When implementing a PMO at this level in the functional organization, remember that small and easy does it! You want to start with one or two projects and gradually expand the influence of the PMO. As project team members begin to see the benefit of the PMO, they will ask for it on other projects. The person or people fulfilling the role of this office should receive basic training in project management activities and in the project tracking that may be used.

Tactical Level

If a PMO were to exist at this level in a functional organization, it is likely that, although it may be called a PMO or some similar name, it is actually focused on the functional area in which it is located. For example, in a manufacturing company, the PMO in marketing will be focused on marketing projects. Generally speaking, the skills of those in this office will be marketing skills and not project management skills.

This PMO may resemble a managerial PMO, but the project managers will report to the director of marketing or vice president of marketing. In any case, the project managers may be very skilled at what they do, and that will be marketing and usually not project management.

We described this relationship in Chapter 2 when we spoke about the difference between a subject matter expert or technical team lead and a project manager. The key to understanding which skill set dominates is to ask a simple question: Would a project manager in this office be able to transfer to another area with the skill set that he or she has? If not, then this person is more likely a subject matter expert or technical team lead.

All the same, if such an office exists within a functional area, even if it is not centered on real project management skills, it could be developed into a PMO with the proper guidance. By developing some of the characteristics of the administrative, center of excellence, and managerial PMO models, it is possible to transform the office into a PMO.

The keys to success would be, first of all, to start small. Begin to work with the best project managers in the area to upgrade their skills in project management. Choose a limited number of projects to begin with, and gradually build up both individuals' skill sets as well as a single, if simple, methodology that all begin to follow.

The second key to success is communication with other functional areas about what is being done. At first, they may not understand what you are doing and resist cooperating. They may even actively work against what you are doing as wasteful and unnecessary. The proof will be in the pudding; as you begin to be more successful in projects, they will begin to want to copy what is happening here. Do not underestimate the resistance, though. It is not unusual for attempts at establishing a PMO and project management in general to fail in a functional

163

organization. Most of all, resist the temptation to use the "training and heroes" route (see In the Real World, "Putting It All Together" in Chapter 8).

Strategic Level

In a purely functional organization, it is highly unlikely that a PMO exists at the strategic level. This is where the brick wall that we spoke about in Chapter 2 comes into play. The wall is often about competition for control and budget between divisions, and as we mentioned in Chapter 2, the intent behind the wall is not to harm the company, although that is frequently the effect.

Although there may be strategic intent and direction in a functional organization, if the strategic direction is not adequately communicated to the tactical level, problems will arise when the projects that are carried out in each functional area do not correspond to strategic direction. Or when they do correspond, the work is duplicated because of a lack of communication among functional areas.

A PMO at this level in a functional organization should have some of the characteristics of the delivery PMO and the administrative-support PMO. A key to success for this PMO would be that, although it may not have complete delivery responsibility of a project, it should be directly responsible for either project initiation or final approval of the project charter for all projects across the firm, when those projects are above a certain level of scope or cost.

Business needs in the project charter stand a better chance of corresponding to the mission and objectives of the firm under this approach. When the project charter is not approved at the highest level of a firm, projects that don't correspond to the mission and business objectives of the firm begin to take up time and money that wastes resources. Eventually, all projects that are above the determined level of scope or cost should be considered at this level with reference only to overall firm objectives. Use of resources would then be based on criteria that affect the entire firm, rather than individual functional areas.

The second key to success for a PMO is in the administrative-support area. It is crucial to the success for the PMO to become the bridge between the strategic and tactical levels of the organization. Without such a bridge, decisions concerning priorities of projects can—and often will—happen within the functional area without reference to the mission and objectives of the firm.

Think back to Frank Coleman's dilemma in Chapter 1. He was constantly shifting resources from one project to another. With no PMO to serve as the crucial link, Frank was basing project priorities on whichever project manager came to see him last (or yelled loudest) about a lack of resources. In the long term, this is a wasteful way to determine project priorities.

Projectized Organization

At the other end of the spectrum is the projectized organization. As we mentioned in Chapter 2, the projectized organization revolves around project management, and the structures are in place to support such an approach. Any work that is not operations (repetitive) is done in projects, with dedicated project teams (see Exhibit 7.3).

Operational Level

In the projectized organization, the person managing the project is a full-time project manager. Although this person may manage more than one project at a time, he or she only manages projects. The roles of technical team lead and subject matter expert are provided by other team members as needed. The project managers would have a considerable amount of authority, including decision-making authority regarding

EXHIBIT 7.3

PMO Characteristics in a Projectized Organization

STO LEVEL	PMO Characteristics in a Projectized Organization			
	Administrative-Support	Center of Excellence	Managerial PMO	Delivery PMO
Operational	✓	✓	✓	✓
Tactical	✓	✓	✓	✓
Strategic	✓	✓	✓	✓

Legend: ✓ Very likely exists ⇔ Somewhat likely exists ✗ Not likely exists

project schedule and project changes. The members of the team report directly to the project manager, rather than to a functional manager.

Project teams last only until a project is completed, at which time the team members are reassigned to another project. Unlike the functional organization, team members do not have jobs in addition to their project work; they are able to focus on the project. The problem in a projectized organization may be that a team member is assigned to several projects at once and may not have adequate time for each. Rather than having a functional manager and a project manager to please, team members may have to please several project managers.

In the projectized organization, a PMO at this level would be an administrative-support PMO. The PMO would be characterized by standardized procedures to support projects and could include individuals who possess skills in that support, the project phases, project tracking, and the use of more sophisticated project tools.

The PMO would employ a standard set of project procedures in supporting projects and would most likely gather information for consolidation and reporting purposes, with the assistance and review of the project manager.

Tactical Level

In the projectized organization, everything is organized around projects. In particular, project managers operate at the tactical level of authority, having a similar level of authority to a functional manager in a functional organization. As a result, there would be a strong PMO at the tactical level of the organization, with several different functions. First, it would have the characteristics of a delivery PMO (i.e., direct responsibility for the delivery of projects). It is possible that the organization is divided into different areas; for example, each area may be responsible for the design and delivery of a particular product or service, and each may have its own PMO that is charged with the delivery of projects.

In addition, there will probably be several centers of excellence, each devoted to its area of technical expertise, including project management. In particular, there are structures in place, in the delivery PMO, to enable communication both horizontally and vertically throughout the organization.

Strategic Level

At the strategic level in a projectized organization, we would expect to have some form of several different PMO models. Because the entire organization is centered on project management, strategic-level direction for project management is a foregone conclusion. Depending on the size of the organization, you could see some differences. For example, in a smaller organization, there may be one single delivery PMO that is on either the strategic or tactical level.

If the PMO is on the tactical level, it would still need to have strong upward communications with strategic authority in the firm, to be certain that projects were aligned with the organization's mission and objectives. If it was on the strategic level, the communications link downward to the tactical level would be crucial. In a larger organization, it is possible that each area within the company has a separate delivery PMO, each reporting to a delivery PMO at the strategic level that would coordinate work between each PMO at the tactical level.

It is probable that a center of excellence PMO would also be on the strategic level. The center of excellence would be working to ensure that best practices are maintained across the organization, as well as trying to provide education and development services to project managers throughout the firm. These project managers would most likely be on a career path in project management, and the center of excellence would ensure that project managers progressed along their career path.

It is likely that there would be a strategic group possibly associated with a PMO that would perform portfolio management (this is the subject of Chapter 8). This group would evaluate all projects within the organization against business mission and objectives, budget constraints, and availability of resources, and then choose which projects would move forward.

The projectized organization is really centered on project management. Is the projectized organization the best possible organization? The answer is perhaps. It is possible that, depending on the industry and the organization's mission and objectives, some other form of organization is the best for that firm.

Matrix Organization

As we saw in Chapter 2, there are three types of matrix organizations: strong, balanced, and weak. The strong matrix organization more closely resembles a projectized organization, and a weak matrix organization more closely resembles a functional organizational. It's safe to say that we can categorize what the PMO in any of these organizations looks like, but in reality there could be a great deal of variation. With that caveat in mind, we will look at each level of all three matrix types at the same time and give a range of characteristics that each may possess, depending where on the scale it falls: strong, balanced, or weak.

Operational Level

You can usually identify where your organization lies between functional and projectized by looking at the project manager. If your project manager is a true project manager with authority to run the project and with team members reporting directly to the project manager, you lean more toward a projectized organization. However, if your project manager does little more than coordinate projects, with little or no authority, you lean more toward a functional organization.

When an organization is undergoing a transformation along the weak-to-strong matrix continuum, the project manager undergoes an interesting transformation. As we move from a weak to a balanced matrix, the project manager transforms from a coordinator to a subject matter expert or a technical team lead. Those firms that are moving from functional to weak to balanced matrix understand the need for some type of project management, but they are focused on product or service as opposed to project. Organizations in transition name project managers as such, but their job descriptions will be preponderantly about subject matter or technical expertise rather than project management, and they will still report to a functional manager. We would suggest that most project managers today fall into this category.

What can we say about the PMO that supports them at the operational level? It would still be focused on administrative support, but as we move toward balanced and strong, it would increase in size and go from merely supporting the administrative work of the project manager and team to having more distinct roles using project management tools and skills. Rather than just doing any administrative work necessary, it would focus on doing specific, project-related activities such as information gathering for status reports, project change control, and project plan updates. The members of the group would have more familiarity with the specific project management tools and software that their firm uses, and they may even be actively involved in supporting different phases of the project (e.g., documenting project planning sessions or attending status meetings).

The question that you want to ask as you develop the project management capability of your organization is: How can I grow the capabilities of this group to support the actual development of project management at the firm? You will always want some lead time in developing skills before they are necessary. For example, if you wish to implement a new project tracking tool, members of the PMO should receive training at the same time as the project managers.

If you are implementing a new project management methodology, members of the PMO need to learn about it at the same time as other members of project teams. By growing the administrative-support PMO in synchronization with the rest of your project management capabilities, you increase your chance of success in project management.

Tactical Level

We have seen that at the operational level, the real transformation from a project coordinator in a functional organization to a project manager in a projectized organization is a change in focus from subject matter or technical expertise to project expertise. The transformation at the tactical level is one of authority—from a coordinator with little authority to a project manager with considerable decision-making and managerial authority.

It would be consistent then to see the PMO at the tactical level also grow along a similar pattern, from an administrative-support PMO (which would still exist at the operational level even in a projectized organization) to a PMO with the characteristics of a delivery and a managerial PMO. In other words, as the project manager's authority grows, so should the authority of the PMO that supports the project manager. There could be several variations on this.

For example, some organizations that are closer to the strong matrix end of the spectrum may have a managerial PMO to which project managers report, but they still may have functional areas that retain ultimate responsibility for the projects. The project manager will have decision-making authority in the project, but not direct-line authority over the team members. The Project Management Institute identifies this type of organization as a composite organization.[1]

A balanced matrix organization may have a project manager with managerial authority, but who still reports to a functional manager. This person probably has a mix of skills, including subject matter or technical and project management. This type of project manager will need the support of a center of excellence to continue progressing in project management.

A center of excellence may exist at the tactical level, but if it does, there is the danger in organizations closer to the weak matrix that the center of excellence might identify more closely with the functional area, because of the difficulty of communicating across functions and the lack of a common language. As the organization approaches the strong matrix, this tendency lessens, because project management becomes the focus.

There is another, less formal entity that can be introduced at the tactical level as well. Mike Shires of Baxter calls it a "community of project management." He describes the entity as a place where project managers throughout the firm can gather to share war stories, discuss best practices, and share experiences. Developing this type of community will help project management practitioners begin to see themselves as professionals in their own right as project managers. In turn, this community also allows the organization to engage project managers in a nonthreatening atmosphere to forward the profession internally and externally with institutions such as the Project Management Institute.

Developing such an entity at the tactical level would require a sponsor and support at the strategic level. Without a broader view, the risk of the community becoming a series of groups concentrating in their own functional area is great.

Strategic Level

At the strategic level, the difference between the functional organization and the projectized organization is the most pronounced. In the functional organization, project management is barely visible, whereas in the projectized organization, project management dominates the scene. As we have frequently mentioned throughout this book, this is where the wall between the strategic and the tactical most likely exists. In a functional organization, projects are handled mostly at the operational and tactical levels.

As we move through the continuum (weak matrix organization to the balanced organization), the wall begins to get lower. Somewhere between the strong matrix organization and the projectized organization, the wall disappears. Between the weak matrix and the balanced matrix, there is little PMO activity at the strategic level. The strategic level of the organization sets the mission and objectives for the firm, but there is inadequate communication between the strategic and the tactical areas.

We mentioned earlier in this chapter that we recommend a functional organization (and this could apply to the weak matrix as well) should have a PMO with some delivery characteristics to ensure strategic input during project initiation. This should be more of a possibility as we arrive at the balanced matrix. Once we move closer to the strong matrix, we will see a PMO with the characteristics of the delivery and managerial PMO. In this way, the link between the firm's mission and objectives and projects becomes more apparent, and two-way communication between the strategic and tactical levels is more possible.

Looking at Your Organization

In order to develop a better understanding of your organization's present circumstances, refer to Chapter 2 to determine what type of organization you have. Once you have determined this, you can use Exhibits 7.1 and 7.2 to determine how well your organization matches up to the models. There is no matrix for matrix organizations; you simply identify those characteristics in the organizational and projectized matrices that apply to your organization.

It is important to remember that a great deal of fluidity exists between these models and the real world. Your organization may seem to be functional, yet you are exhibiting some characteristics of a more advanced PMO structure at the tactical level. If that is so, congratulations! It is also possible that you may be a balanced matrix organization, but some PMO functions are still at a weak matrix of functional level. There is no reason to despair; change is possible, if sometimes difficult. What is important is to recognize the difficulty and begin implementing a solution.

Summary

In this chapter, we have reviewed the different types of project management offices and why project management offices may take so many different forms. We have explored how a firm's structure affects the project management office and how the STO model affects the project management office. Finally, we have provided tools to help you analyze your organization and identify the characteristics for a project management office for any area within your organization.

Endnote

1. *A Guide to the Project Management Body of Knowledge* (Newton Square, PA: Project Management Institute, 2000), p. 23.

CHAPTER 8

Project Portfolio Management

After reading this chapter you will be able to

- Understand what project portfolio management is
- Understand how project portfolio management relates to organizational strategy
- Understand the three purposes and processes of project portfolio management
- Understand what a balanced portfolio is
- Understand how to maximize the value of your firm's project portfolio

Why Project Portfolio Management?

Think about your own experience at any of the companies you have worked for over the years. Have you ever been working on a project of some sort that was intended to either correct a major problem or create an important advance within the organization? As you began to work on the project and drew resources from within the organization, you began to bump into people in other areas of the organization who looked at what you were doing and said, "Hey, wait a minute. I'm supposed to be working on that!"

What often ensued was a discussion about who should be working on what, who had authority, and who should be working on the project.

What may have ensued, particularly in functional and weak matrix organizations (although other types of organizations are not immune), was a full-scale turf war about which area is responsible for working on that project. Almost as frequently, one area wins out over another. In reality, everyone loses. To understand why, let's look at a phenomenon called fractals.

Fractals[1] are computer-generated images that flow from the plotting of mathematical equations. An interesting phenomenon of fractals is that they contain replicas of themselves. If you were to look closer at a fractal, you would begin to see exact replicas of the fractal contained within the fractal. No matter how great a magnification you used, you would never get to the end of the fractal; you would always see more replicas within replicas (see Exhibit 8.1).

EXHIBIT 8.1

Fractal

Source: © 2003, Derek Simeone, Bluespeed, *www.bluespeed9.com.*

A company is like a fractal; if a problem or a characteristic is perceived in one area of the company, the same problem or characteristic will often be perceived in other areas as well. Those who perceive the problem are working at a very high level of magnification; that is, they are seeing the problem at a close range as it affects them. It is normal that they do not perceive the existence of the same problem or characteristic in other areas of the organization.

The mistake they make is in how they interpret and react to the discovery of others working on the same problem or characteristic in another area of the firm. Rather than developing territoriality around the project, the individuals should see these discoveries as being important for the organization. In reality, it is difficult for individuals who are working at one project level to have a higher-level vision to see the bigger picture.

Earlier in the book, we discussed the difference between a project manager and a subject matter expert or technical team lead. It is very difficult to work as a project manager and a technical team lead at the same time, because each role demands a different level of detail; the technical team lead works at a detailed level within the project, whereas the project manager works at a higher level, seeing that tasks were completed as planned and keeping a finger on the project's pulse.

In the same way, a project manager cannot see what is happening at an enterprise level. Astute project managers can get a sense of what is happening based on what they see around them (e.g., multiple "Hey, I'm working on that!" experiences is a clue) and alert a higher level within the organization.

That higher level of vision is the purpose of project portfolio management (abbreviated PPM and also known as enterprise project management, or EPM). If we look at all that we have covered in this book, PPM is the last element to complete the picture. So far, we have covered the basic mechanics of project management, the five phases of project management. We have also covered project management maturity and the project management office (PMO). These subjects all answer the question, "How do you do project management?"

We have also stressed the importance of strategic project management (i.e., linking the objectives of a project with the mission and objectives of the organization). In this chapter, we answer the question, "Why do you use project management?" In essence, project management is a strategic tool to carry an organization's mission and objectives forward. The PMO ensures, at various levels of the organization, that project management is employed professionally and that projects are being done according to plan. PPM ensures that the right projects are being done to achieve the organization's mission and objectives.

Project Portfolio Management

In Chapter 2, we defined strategic project management as "the use of the appropriate project management knowledge, skills, tools, and techniques in the context of the Company's goals and objectives, so that the project deliverables will contribute to Company value in a way that can be measured." In a similar fashion, we define project portfolio management as "the use of the appropriate management knowledge, skills, tools, and techniques to maximize the alignment of the Company's project portfolio with the Company's goals and objectives." Just as projects contribute to the company's success by producing deliverables that add measurable value, so PPM contributes to success by ensuring that the company is doing the right projects to begin with.

PPM is a key component of strategic project management. As with project management, many tools (both software and other) can assist in PPM. We again emphasize that the installation of a software tool does not constitute PPM.

In order to better understand how PPM fits into the big picture, think back to the story of Frank Coleman in Chapter 1. Frank was run ragged by all of the problems he was experiencing. When he first brought in a consultant, he thought that the solution to his problem was to train everyone in project management. As the consultant pointed out in their first conversation, Frank's problems could not be corrected by project management training alone. PPM was also a part of Frank's problem.

If you recall, Frank's method of prioritizing projects was based on who came to him with the biggest crisis. He did not have a comprehensive view of the entire portfolio of projects that ABC Corp. faced, and he was constantly putting out fires. Nor did he have a good idea of how the mix of projects was affecting the firm. He did not even have a good idea of what projects really cost, given constant overruns, so that it would be very difficult to develop budgets around projects.

Frank prioritized projects around crises, which really meant that there were no priorities at all. Improving project management could help make ABC Corp. more efficient and is probably part of the solution for this fictitious company. However, improvements in project management cannot solve the lack of project priorities from which ABC Corp. suffered. It is very difficult for one person to prioritize projects for anything except a very small organization, and it's impossible in a large organization.

PPM requires information from all levels of the organization. Only PPM can truly help this situation.

Purposes and Processes of Project Portfolio Management

PPM has three purposes:

1. To link all projects to the company's strategy
2. To balance the portfolio of projects the company is undertaking
3. To maximize the value of the portfolio

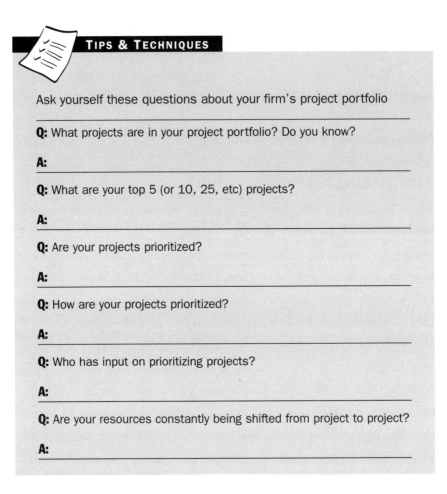

TIPS & TECHNIQUES

Ask yourself these questions about your firm's project portfolio

Q: What projects are in your project portfolio? Do you know?

A:

Q: What are your top 5 (or 10, 25, etc) projects?

A:

Q: Are your projects prioritized?

A:

Q: How are your projects prioritized?

A:

Q: Who has input on prioritizing projects?

A:

Q: Are your resources constantly being shifted from project to project?

A:

Attaining a strategic view and choosing and executing the correct projects achieve the three purposes and, therefore, constitute the three processes of portfolio management. Let us take a closer look at the purposes and processes.

Link to Strategy

The first purpose of PPM is to link the project portfolio to the company's strategy. It goes without saying that an organization without a strategy is likely to have a chaotic portfolio of projects. Even when a well-developed strategy exists, it is often difficult to link projects across the organization to the strategy. Let's take an example to illustrate linking strategy and project portfolio—a company that produces nondurable goods for the retail market.

Let us also suppose that at the present time, there is a growth market for certain of the goods the company could produce, but it does not have the full capacity to produce as many of these goods as the market will absorb. The company must undergo some rapid growth in order to increase capacity to meet the rising demand. We must then look across the company's portfolio of projects, those being undertaken and those being proposed, to see if these projects support the firm's present strategic direction. The key here is to look over the entire project portfolio, not just those projects that seem to directly affect the effort.

Obviously, you would consider any project that increases production capacity, such as reconfiguring equipment or acquiring new capacity. You would also want to coordinate between all function areas, such as a project that aims to develop marketing strategy for the new product would probably also fall into a higher priority. There may be other, less obvious ways that projects could affect the strategy. For example, it might seem that spending time, effort, and money on new human resource information technology might not be appropriate.

By the same token, if there are expectations for rapid growth, upgrading the human resources information systems might enable HR personnel to better cope with hiring a large number of employees efficiently, which could support the strategy. A project that would enable computer-based, self-paced learning for a large number of new employees might also support the strategy. However, a project to redevelop an older product that does not have a large market share or does not show the potential of the new product may be better off delayed or cancelled.

If you think back to Frank Coleman's story, because he had no strategic view, his only criteria for prioritizing projects was how loudly the client complained. Consider the complaints that Amanda Stevens, the VP of Manufacturing at Bigelow Company, made about the delay in a prototype. Amanda Stevens considered herself a good client, but we have no definition of a good client. We do know that the prototype was delayed because of constant requests from Bigelow to make changes.

Let's put Amanda Stevens and Bigelow Company in the context of our previous example. What if Bigelow represented a product that was in a mature market, without a lot of growth potential and, in addition, Bigelow was demanding changes that did not significantly improve the value of the product. Should they be given as high a priority as they were in the opening story? Probably not. Again linking the previous example with our opening chapter, if the HR project that Frank borrowed resources from was actually supporting the system upgrade to facilitate a large number of new hires for the new product, delaying this project may cause more harm to the overall strategy than to continue to delay a prototype for a product that no longer represented the company's future. As you can see, the real key to linking projects to strategy is by linking projects throughout the entire company, including internal projects, to the strategy. For an excellent example of how an organization used project management to change, take a look at In the Real World, "Creating Strategic Change."

Balanced Portfolio

When we speak of a balanced portfolio, you may ask the question, "balanced between what and what?" That is exactly the question. The answer is a bit more difficult, however; it really depends on the company and its mission and objectives. One of the classic balances that some

Creating Strategic Change

Strategic project management is a tool for creating change in an organization. Change can be internal (affecting the structure or operations of an organization) or external (where the organization interacts with the public, such as marketing and product development). Whenever there is change in an organization, strategic project management can provide the framework to facilitate that change.

An excellent case in point is the Field Museum of Natural History in Chicago, which is one of the premier institutions of its kind in the United States. As with many organizations, the role of information technology expanded gradually over the years at the Field Museum. Originally, different types of computer systems and programs were initiated ad hoc to support the scientific mission of the Field Museum. But at the turn of the twenty-first century, the Field Museum found itself with a great variety of systems used not only for scientific purposes but also for business and administrative functions. Many of the systems were older legacy systems, and providing proper support was very difficult. In addition, the various internal clients of the Field Museum were not all happy with the technology management situation.

The Field Museum hired Bill Barnett as its Chief Information Officer. Working with Project Manager Julie Brubaker, Bill set about creating change. In this case, change involved organizationally transforming a legacy Computer Services department into a best-practices-based Information Technology service. Change is never easy, and a major change in an institution steeped in a long and rich tradition can be very difficult, even if all involved agree on the necessity of change. This type of change project would require particular care in the initiation and planning phases in order to maximize the chances of success.

The first challenge was to link the project to the strategic mission and objectives of the Field Museum. This was a formidable challenge because the very nature of the former Computer Services department

IN THE REAL WORLD CONTINUED

had changed. Originally founded to support the scientific mission of the museum, this department now had responsibility for mission-critical business applications as well as important infrastructure and support to their internal clients as a priority. In addition, they were being challenged to work better in partnership with their internal clients about information systems.

Bill and Julie understood early on the importance of communication in this type of change project. They communicated early and often, holding Town Hall Meetings to convey information and gather feedback. They needed their audience of clients to understand the new mandate and how it would affect them. Bill and Julie also wanted to collect the needs of their clients.

Julie developed a multiphase project plan that emphasized communication. The plan had six phases, and it is interesting to note that the first four phases were all part of the initial planning and development process. The iterative planning approach, coupled with extensive communication and feedback, allowed Julie to help the Field Museum staff understand the new Information Technology organization mandate, and participate in the development and review of the new organizational structure that would be put in place:

- *Phase 1.* Business needs analysis and initial communication
- *Phase 2.* Define basic organizational structure
- *Phase 3.* Define detailed structure and individual roles
- *Phase 4.* Define major tasks, processes, and procedures
- *Phase 5.* Communication and rollout of new structure
- *Phase 6.* Postimplementation review and determination of ongoing projects

By taking ample time to plan this project, success—although difficult—was achieved. Julie Brubaker's decision to construct the project phases in this manner is a great example of how an organization companies look at is between risk and reward; in other words, how large a risk are they willing to take in order to receive a certain reward or benefit for the risk.

Other balances may be between internal and external projects, cost cutting and development, spending on technology and spending on bricks and mortar. Chances are that your portfolio balance will be uniquely yours, depending on your company's strategy, goals, and objectives. Most often, a portfolio will be balanced between more than two different factors.

A good example of balancing a portfolio occurred at Herman Miller, an innovative office furniture manufacturer. Faced with a downturn in its market, Herman Miller was forced to examine its business carefully to decide how to deal with the situation. The senior management team was trying to find a way to cut costs without cutting the heart out of the business.

For guidance, executives returned to the company's mission—helping customers "Create Great Places to Work." They first established a working framework for their considerations, including strategic, financial, and cultural considerations. Beginning with the question, "Who do we want to be?" management realized that innovation was always at the center of their strategy, so they decided early on that research and development funds would be off limits.

Their thinking was that if they created a leaner and more efficient company, but did not have new and innovative products for the marketplace, then all the work could be for naught. The company realized that Herman Miller's great strength was its ability to innovate. To do anything to impede or diminish this ability would harm the business. Other expenses would be cut, but in order to prepare for competition in a difficult market, as well as a future economic turnaround, Herman Miller must preserve and strengthen its innovation engine.

In addition, management also brought in another aspect of balance that we mentioned previously: risk and reward; that is, carefully considering the risk benefit of actions that Herman Miller would take. The strategy worked, because Herman Miller subsequently increased efficiency while decreasing its actual manufacturing space by a significant level. Herman Miller is now poised to take innovations to new arenas such as "Places to Heal."

Maximize Value

Maximizing the value of a project portfolio depends on linking that portfolio to the company's strategy effectively and putting into place a decision or phase-gate process that will compare projects in the portfolio against strategy and balance. Only those projects that are aligned with strategy, fit within the correct balance, and represent the maximum return should be approved (we discuss the decision process later in this chapter). The most frequently used value for judging projects is profitability, although profitability can make it more difficult to judge internal projects when there is no direct link between the project and the company's bottom line.

An example of an internal project that may be difficult to quantify according to profitability would be the TAP Pharmaceuticals example in Chapter 4 (In the Real World, "Mitigating Risk with Communications"). Improving human resource processes does not connect directly to the profitability of the company. An indirect link to profitability could be established through cost. TAP had just come through a period of rapid expansion and wanted to increase productivity within human resources without augmenting staff. By rationalizing business processes, the company enabled human resources to provide services to more employees without increasing staff.

Additionally, part of TAP's strategic objective was to provide a great place to work, thus minimizing staff turnover, which would also have a certain cost. In this way, the HR process improvement project could be justified by several criteria: contributing to the bottom line and alignment with company strategy.

Maximizing the value of a project portfolio also highlights the need to keep project planning and budgeting closely aligned. Having a corporate strategy in place is a good thing; however, if the budget does not support the strategy, then the strategy is nothing more than a showpiece or a corporate wish. As mentioned earlier, Herman Miller wanted to continue as an innovator in the marketplace, even while it needed to cut costs because of the market being down during the recent recession. Research and development is costly, and it would have been easy to reduce costs in that area. Realizing that the budget had to support the strategy, however, Herman Miller made the research and development budget untouchable, thereby supporting Herman Miller's corporate strategy.

Attaining a Strategic View

The overall process of PPM could be compared to a funnel. Attaining a strategic view, the first step in PPM can be represented by the large end of the funnel. All projects in the organization are collected in the large end of the funnel. As the projects proceed down the funnel, they are submitted to a process of evaluation of the factors we have discussed. At the far end of the funnel emerge the projects that are actually going to be executed (see Exhibit 8.2).

The process begins with the submission of all projects to the portfolio management process. Depending on the maturity of the process and the manner in which the organization operates, projects can be submitted either at the idea stage, before any significant work has been done, or at the end of initiation, in which case the project charter has been completed, the project sponsor and business need are identified,

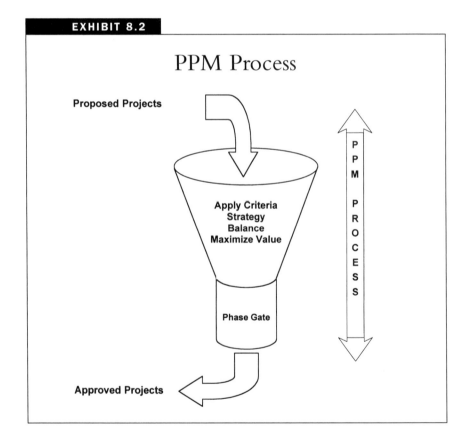

EXHIBIT 8.2

PPM Process

Proposed Projects

Apply Criteria
Strategy
Balance
Maximize Value

Phase Gate

Approved Projects

P P M P R O C E S S

high-level deliverables are defined, and a preliminary project cost estimate is made.

The difference between submission before or after project initiation has several ramifications. Submission before initiation is less costly because the use of resources, time, and money are minimal. Projects submitted after initiation have made a more significant investment in time, resources, and money that is not subject to budgeting as part of the portfolio process. However, submission after initiation provides more detailed information to be used in considering the project.

Some organizations require submission before initiation and have a more liberal policy about initiating any project they consider to be viable. They also do not expect all projects that are initiated to actually be executed. They would consider the cost of initiating the projects as an opportunity cost. In some firms, projects under a certain dollar value and duration are exempt from the portfolio process. In these cases, the budget for performing the projects would come directly from the budget of the functional area executing the project, rather than from the budget controlled by strategic planners.

Choosing Projects

Choosing the projects for a project portfolio simply means applying the criteria that have been established by strategy, balance, and maximizing value concerns of the organization. It sounds simple, but the process may be quite complex. The key to success is to have clearly defined measures against which each project must be evaluated and given a value. The values would prioritize the projects in order of the criteria. The projects would then be evaluated according to budget criteria and resources available to schedule an actual project start date. Many PPM processes also include regular evaluations of projects in execution to consider whether to continue execution.

Let's go back to Frank Coleman and ABC Corp., at a later time when they have implemented PPM and see what they are doing. They have formed a project portfolio evaluation group, made up of Frank, the COO, the CFO, and the heads of various functional areas. This group meets regularly to review projects. In the case of ABC Corp., the group looks at projects after initiation, but before planning and execution begin. All projects must return to the group after each phase in order to get approval for continuation. For each project, the project sponsor must present to the group, accompanied by the project manager, if one has already been appointed. At times, members of the project portfolio evaluation group may also be sponsoring a project. Involving the project sponsor directly in the portfolio process has improved communication between the tactical level of the various areas and the strategic level of the company. Project sponsors are now more directly involved in their projects and must support them well to win approval.

The evaluation group first ranks all projects on a risk–reward basis, using the risk–reward quadrangle. According to the criteria that ABC Corp. has set, projects that have no more than medium risk, but medium to high return, are given the highest priority. Projects that are too risky or with a very low return are eliminated at this point. Projects are then listed in a spreadsheet according to the initial ranking. Next the evaluation group considers strategic importance and gives each project a rating based on how well it corresponds to ABC Corp.'s strategy. After adding in the second factor, the prioritized list of projects often has different rankings for some projects. For example, a particular project may seem to present a good possibility based on risk–reward criteria, but if it does not correspond as well in alignment with ABC Corp.'s strategy, it may move down in the rankings (see Exhibit 8.3).

Next, the evaluation group looks at the budget allocations that have been established based on the company's strategy and chooses the projects that give the best return based on budget allocation. For example, if ABC Corp. were pursuing a growth strategy that necessitated upgrading manufacturing equipment, it would allocate a certain portion of the annual budget to that purpose. If growth were a high priority in the strategy, then a project that addresses the business need would also have a higher priority when allocating budget to projects. Again, the order of projects on the list may change after the budget allocation is considered.

Finally, ABC Corp. would look at available resources in order to schedule the actual start date of projects. For example, it may be possible that the top-priority project demands so many resources that it cannot be started right away, but a lower-ranked project demands fewer resources and can be started sooner. In this case, it would make sense for the evaluation group to sanction the lower-priority project to begin immediately and the higher-priority project to start at a later date when sufficient resources are available.

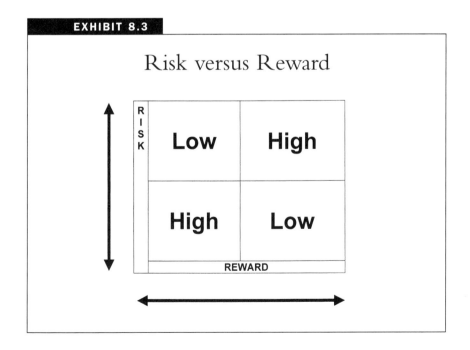

EXHIBIT 8.3

Risk versus Reward

The portfolio evaluation group at ABC Corp. does not end its work when a project is sanctioned to begin. The group also evaluates project execution to ensure that the projects are adhering to schedule, budget, and deliverables, and that projects are continuing to correspond to ABC Corp.'s strategy. For example, after detailed project planning is completed, the project sponsor and project manager return to the evaluation group to present the project plan for approval. At the end of each subsequent phase of the project, the sponsor and project manager report to the evaluation group for approval of continuation.

The evaluation group acts to ensure that projects meet their goals and support strategy in order to receive funding. At the same time, the urgency of different projects encourages the evaluation group to act quickly to evaluate ongoing projects. The criteria that the fictional ABC Corp. uses within its evaluation group are just an example. Each organization must choose criteria that are appropriate for its strategy and situation. The order in which projects are evaluated and the manner in which the portfolio management process takes place will be different for each company.

Implementing Project Portfolio Management

The foundation for implementing project portfolio information within an organization is the existence of project management at some level within the organization. We feel that the optimum circumstance is to have implemented strategic project management. If we refer again to the STO solution model, the solution for many of the real problems within an organization is strategic project management. Strategic project management depends on breaking down the walls that exist between the strategic, tactical, and operational levels of the organization (see Exhibit 1.2).

PPM also depends not only on the walls being broken down between the levels of an organization, but also between the various areas of an organization. Also, each of the organization types that we have introduced presents a different level of challenge to PPM. Let's look at what the challenges might be.

Functional Organization

As you will recall, a functional organization is organized into divisions and departments, each with its own authority structure and chain of command. We have already seen that implementing project management was challenging because it represented a cross-divisional focus that was foreign to the organization. A similar challenge exists for PPM because of the budget and planning process that is most likely in place. In the functional organization, budgets and planning usually start from the bottom up.

At some point, a consolidated budget is created at a higher level of the organization and communicated back down to the organization. Each division is competing for dollars, but often without a great deal of knowledge about what is happening in other divisions. This type of budgeting process also encourages a "use it or lose it" mentality in the divisions. If you do not use up your budget this year, showing that it was really needed, then you will lose some of it the next year.

Introducing PPM can be challenging in this situation, because it is taking a vision across the entire firm. There is likely to be resistance among lower-level management and employees. Whereas executive and upper-level management see PPM as a way to plan and budget for the entire organization, lower-level managers and employees may see it as something being taken away. Implementing PPM in a functional organization requires that project management be implemented, at least at a basic level, for all projects within a division. Having project management in place would provide the required information necessary for PPM: project charters and project plans providing information about the time and resources needed to accomplish projects and status reporting providing the actual results to be used in decision making are examples of required information.

As a first step, PPM could be implemented in each division. The division would be allocated a budget for the year. Next, an evaluation group would develop the PPM process for the division. Care must be taken to guide the development process because the eventual goal is to promote the PPM process to the strategic level. You must be sure that each divisional evaluation team uses the same set of principles to guide its decisions. If the walls are not broken down, according to the STO solution model, this will be very difficult to accomplish.

When the PPM process is functioning well in each division, you can then bridge the divisional processes together on a strategic level. You may decide to keep divisional evaluation groups in place but streamline the process for the strategic level. It is important to remember that the divisional groups will only decide on what is important within their own budgets. They are not able to decide that a project that is relatively high on the divisional priority list may actually be much lower when viewed strategically across the entire organization.

The divisional evaluation group would move ahead with its project, while the strategic evaluation group would not. Again, the challenge in the functional organization is to gradually change the vision at the tactical and operational levels to a strategic vision.

Projectized Organization

It will be much easier to implement PPM in a projectized organization because all of the supporting features are already in place. The walls have been broken down between the strategic, tactical, and operational levels, and communications flow throughout the organization. Projects are developed according to the five phases of project management and are tracked appropriately.

The projectized organization has archives of information that can be used to plan projects. There is most likely a PMO or several PMOs playing different types of directing and supporting roles. It is quite possible that the only major challenge to implementing PPM in a projectized organization will be to determine what the relationship is between the PMO and the PPM evaluation group.

It is quite possible that a managerial PMO may already be doing PPM, in which case it would be necessary to delineate the difference between the two bodies. Remember, the PPM evaluating group approves projects and the managerial PMO executes projects.

Matrix Organization

As we originally said in Chapter 3, the strong matrix organization more closely resembles the projectized organization, whereas the balanced matrix organization takes its characteristics almost equally from the projectized and functional organizations and the weak matrix organization is much closer to the functional organization. The approach to implementing PPM in a matrix organization will depend on the type of matrix organization with which you are dealing. The strong matrix organization will lend itself well to PPM, whereas the weak matrix organization will require more effort. As with the functional organization, the weak matrix will probably require developing the rudiments of project management before actually implementing PPM. The key to success will be to determine which of the pieces of the project management foundation are missing, and being sure to implement the foundation before initiating PPM. It would be safe to say that any organization that does not have at least a rudimentary foundation in project management would be building a house on sand to implement PPM before project management. Just as you can't implement a PMO when there is nothing to manage, you cannot implement PPM if you do not have sufficient information about the portfolio to manage it.

Bringing It All Together

We opened this book with a story about the travails of Frank Coleman, the Chief Operating Officer of ABC Corp. In closing, let's look in on Frank some three years later (we don't want to discourage you, but it is realistic to set a timeline of three to five years to implement a project management solution that includes a PMO and PPM).

Frank walked into his office at about 6:30 A.M. Even though things were working much better now, Frank still liked to get into the office early; maybe he's just an early bird. As he walked into his office, he saw 10 or 12 notes on his chair and keyboard, nothing like the dozens that he used to find every day. The light was flashing on his telephone, but even that was no longer daunting because he knew there would only be a handful of messages.

He started up his computer, and when it was ready, he went to his project dashboard to see what was going on. It was Monday morning, so he expected to see the results of the status reports from all of his project managers. The hard work they had all put in—learning and adapting a methodology that really worked, long hours of mentoring that helped his people finally understand what project management was all about—had been worth it. He no longer cringed on Monday morning to see what crisis was coming up.

Frank could look at his project dashboard and see in a few minutes where the problems were. Noting red lights on six projects indicating potential problems, he made notes to talk to those project managers today to find out what was wrong and see if he should be calling the clients. He liked that approach a lot better, talking to clients before there was actually a problem. There were still things that slipped through the cracks, but that was the exception now, not the rule.

The new PMO was working out well, and some people were actually asking about becoming project managers. His own project managers were starting to feel proud about what they did. Three years ago, nobody wanted to know anything about being a project manager.

The project evaluation group was working out well, too. Frank was so glad that he was not responsible all by himself for determining which project was the highest priority. He would never forget the series of spreadsheets he saw over the first nine months that they worked on implementing project management. Where had all those projects come from? Most of them he had never heard of, let alone approved. Different groups were working on similar initiatives for the same clients without even knowing it. They had eliminated a huge amount of waste, and the company was now functioning at a better level of efficiency than ever, without hiring any new personnel.

Best of all, he no longer had to fend off Jim Barnett, the CEO, who always had a pet project he was pushing. The evaluation group had made a real difference in persuading Jim that some of his projects were just not good for the company. Sure, things weren't perfect, but they were a lot better than they ever were before. Endings like this don't just happen in a book; they happen in real life. In the Real World, "Putting It All Together," demonstrates how it is really done.

You may say that it is very easy to write a rosy finish to Frank's story, and you would be right. However, if you were to go back through the book and look at each of the stories about real companies and real people, you should quickly conclude that strategic project management can work for you and your organization. It will take a lot of hard work, but you will find that the real benefits will far outweigh the investment in time, money, and resources that you will make along the way. We sincerely wish you great success in "getting things done!"

Putting It All Together

Creating a more projectized organization does not happen overnight. The type of organization that you are dealing with, the organization's industry, and business structure all have an effect on how project management will be developed. A very important element in the implementation of project management, particularly in a large organization, is a paradox. On the one hand, there must be strong executive sponsorship for the effort, but on the other hand, the effort must begin at the grass-roots level. To better explain, let's take a look at the experiences of Baxter International, Inc., a pharmaceuticals company.

Several years ago, the Baxter executive management team, consisting of the Chief Executive Officer, Chief Financial Officer, the heads of each of Baxter's four business units, and several others, became aware that there was a skills gap in project management. Their conclusion, based on experiences with research and development, new products, and other types of projects led them to bring Michael Shires into the organization as the Director of Project Management. Baxter's executive management team fulfilled the first half of the paradox correctly: Mike reports directly to a member of the executive team, ensuring good communication and indicating strong sponsorship by the team.

Many felt that this was a training issue, and they wanted to create training for those who were managing projects as well as to hire several experienced senior project managers to lead the way. Although Mike agreed that training was needed, he also understood the other half of the paradox: the need to start at the grass-roots level to build a project management organization.

In addition to leveraging the expertise of Baxter Institute (i.e., the internal training and development service), in order to initiate a training program, Mike began to develop a project management organization. At the grass-roots level, Mike began to build a community of practice for project management across the business. This gave project managers from different business units the opportunity to meet and share ideas and information about project management. Of particular importance is how this community began to help project managers across the firm to develop their identity as project managers, as well as to trade information about best practices and tools and techniques that worked at Baxter.

Mike instituted monthly brown bag lunches for project managers in different locations. The lunches were varied in nature, at times having speakers and at others simply having discussions among the project managers. Baxter also used technology to bring the group together, allowing a speaker in one location to address all of the various groups across the country. Mike also began holding quarterly meetings of all project management personnel. Baxter has gradually built up a community of 150 project managers. This group offers the kind of connections that can be leveraged across the firm.

Baxter's project management office added to its role by beginning to function as a center of excellence, cataloging best practices and encouraging their use. They have focused on the use of more standard practices in Research and Development across the different business units of the company.

Baxter's project management office took on another role: the process of prioritizing projects. This initiative worked through the executive management team, which designated the most important projects as Baxter Top Projects. Once a project was so recognized, it was given firmwide priority. This was a major achievement in our tural change within Baxter and helped distinguish among the projects that were most important to the business and any other project, including "stealth" projects.

At this point, the Baxter project management office had accomplished several significant achievements:

- It provided the link between the executive management team and the rest of the firm, so that everyone understood which projects were important.

- It served as a center of excellence, working to get project managers the skills necessary to succeed.

- It served as a center of expertise, with input in the planning, resource scheduling, and risk assessment of projects.

- It created a benchmark on the probability of getting a project to the finish. The project budget now serves more as a placeholder than a guarantee. You must get through the gates successfully to continue funding.

The Baxter project management office has begun serving as portfolio management center in two stages. First, planning was attached more to the budget process. Each business prioritized not only their Top Baxter Projects, but also other projects, and indicated where the limit was for project funding in a business unit. In the second stage, Baxter took a more strategic approach. Portfolio management was connected to the strategic objectives of the firm. Projects were prioritized across the firm, based on their strategic importance.

Several years later, the signs of success include a project management office structure that is replicated within each business unit, to which that unit's project managers report. Each business unit project management office handles the day-to-day work of project management in the business, and the original project management office remains the center of excellence. Data collected indicates that milestone achievement rate has improved, and many projects that do not meet the standards for research and development are terminated earlier in their life cycle, saving money for other research. Baxter is now well positioned to begin working on project management maturity.

Endnote

1. For more information on fractals and chaos theory, consult Margaret J. Wheatley, *Leadership and the New Science: Discovering Order in a Chaotic World Revised* (San Francisco: Berrett-Koehler Publishing, 2001).

Index

U

Unknowns, 104

W

Walls within companies, 48–51, 192, 194
  benefits of breaking down, 51
WBS. *See* Work breakdown structure
Work breakdown structure, 75–79
  and estimating cost, resources, and time,
    76
  and project change control, 76
  benefits, 76